D1045913

# AUTHORITY

# Richard Sennett

# Authority

**Vintage Books**
A Division of Random House • New York

First Vintage Books Edition, February 1981
Copyright © 1980 by Richard Sennett
All rights reserved under International and Pan-American
Copyright Conventions. Published in the United States by
Random House, Inc., New York, and in Canada by Random
House of Canada Limited, Toronto. Originally published by
Alfred A. Knopf, Inc., New York, in April 1980.

Grateful acknowledgment is made to the Harvard Business
Review for permission to reprint an excerpt from "The
Dynamics of Subordinancy" by Abraham Zaleznik (May-June
1965). Copyright © 1965 by the President and Fellows of
Harvard College. All rights reserved. Reprinted by permission
of the Harvard Business Review.

Library of Congress Cataloging in Publication Data
Sennett, Richard, 1943-
Authority.
Reprint of the 1st ed. published by
Knopf, New York.
1. Authority. I. Title.
[HM271.S36 1981]   303.3'6   80-6125
ISBN 0-394-74655-4

Manufactured in the United States of America

Front-of-cover painting by Jacques Louis David,
The Oath of the Horatii. Courtesy of the Chefs d'Oeuvre
du Musée du Louvre.

AC0154

For Dorothy Sennett

*I am that father whom your boyhood lacked and suffered pain for lack of. I am he.*

*This is not princely, to be swept away by wonder at your father's presence. No other Odysseus will ever come, for he and I are one, the same. . . .*

*Odyssey,* Book XVI,
translated by Robert Fitzgerald

# Contents

# Acknowledgements

This book began as a Sigmund Freud Memorial Lecture at the University of London in 1977. I wish to thank the trustees of the Lectureship, and in particular Professor Richard Wollheim, for inviting me. Subsequent research and writing of this book were made possible by a grant from the National Science Foundation.

Many friends helped me with advice and criticism. I would like to thank especially Susan Sontag, Loren Baritz, Thomas Kuhn, Daniel Bell, David Rieff, Rosalind Krauss, Anthony Giddens, and David Kalstone.

As always, Robert Gottlieb and the staff of Alfred A. Knopf, Inc. have been sympathetic and efficient.

R.S.

# AUTHORITY

# Introduction

This book is the first of four related essays on the emotional bonds of modern society. I want to understand how people make emotional commitments to one another, what happens when these commitments are broken or absent, and the social forms these bonds take. It is easier to see the emotional commitments made in a family than in a factory, but the emotional life of a large milieu is equally real. Without ties of loyalty, authority, and fraternity, no society as a whole, and none of its institutions, could long function. Emotional bonds therefore have political consequences. They often knit people together against their own interests, as when a people feel loyalty to a charismatic leader who takes away their liberty. Occasionally the need for satisfying emotional relations will turn people against institutions they feel are inadequate. Such complex relations between psychology and politics are the subject matter of the four books in this study.

The present essay is about authority; the second will be

about solitude, the third about fraternity, the fourth about ritual. The bond of authority is built of images of strength and weakness; it is the emotional expression of power. Solitude is the perception of being cut off from other people, of a bond missing. Fraternity is based on images of likeness; it is an emotion elicited by the sense of "us," nationally, sexually, politically. Ritual is the most passionate, least self-conscious bond of all; it is an emotional unity achieved through drama. As the overall project progresses, I shall correlate these four subjects, but each book is intended as an independent essay.

The word "bond" has a double meaning. It is a connection; it is also, as in "bondage," a constraint. No child could prosper without the sense of trust and nurturance which comes from believing in the authority of its parents, yet in adult life it is often feared that the search for these emotional benefits of authority will turn people into docile slaves. Similarly, fraternity is a connection among adults which can easily become a nightmare: it can provoke either hostile aggression against outsiders or an internal struggle about who "really" belongs. Solitude seems a lack of connection and therefore a lack of constraint. But it can be so painful that people will blindly commit themselves to a marriage, a job, or a community, and yet find that in the midst of others they remain alone. A ritual unifies, but the sentiment of unity is strange because it disappears the moment the ritual ends.

One result of the ambiguity of emotional bonds is that they are seldom stable. That instability is captured in the root meaning of the term "emotion." Aristotle, in *De Anima,* spoke of emotion as the principle of movement in human experience; the Latin root of the word is *movere,* "to move." But the origins of the word also suggest a larger meaning for emotion than sheer instability. Change occurs in what we feel, Aristotle wrote, because jealousy, anger, and compassion are the results of sensations reflected upon. They are not just sensations; they are sensations we have thought about. This process allows us to act in the world, to affect and to change it. Were we not to feel, we would not be fully awake, Aristotle wrote, and very little would happen in our lives.

This seemingly common-sense notion has not been a dominant one in the history of psychology. Many of Aristotle's contemporaries thought emotions were visited on men by the gods; this view reappeared in the Middle Ages, so that lust was the voice of the Devil speaking, compassion an echo of God's voice of love for man, and so on. Descartes wrote a treatise on emotion which revived Aristotle's ideas, but most of his scientific contemporaries were replacing medieval superstitions with concepts of emotion as purely physiological states, as in the idea of bodily "humors." Modern psychology, up to quite recently, was prone to separate cognition and affect, thinking and emotion. In its early history, psychoanalysis had a poorly developed theory of emotions, and the range of emotions in the psychoanalytic vocabulary was more primitive than the range of emotions in an ordinary adult's experience.

All this has changed in the last generation; Aristotle's view that emotion is a joint product of sensing and thinking has again come to the fore in various ways. In continental psychology, this view appears in the work of Jean Piaget, in the Anglo-Saxon world in the writings of Jerome Bruner. In psychoanalysis, this unified view dominates the writings of Roy Schafer and Charles Rycroft. Philosophic interest in the concept of emotion was reawakened by Suzanne K. Langer's *Mind: An Essay on Human Feeling,* and explored in more disciplined ways in many of the writings of Jean-Paul Sartre. It could be said of this new view generally that it seeks to understand anger, jealousy, and compassion as interpretations people make of events or other people. The sense of this in English is conveyed by the question "What do you feel about him?" Judgement and reasoning are ingredients in coming to have "feelings about" another person. There is also a moral dimension to this psychological view. Images like blind passion or blind ambition suggest the person feeling them was so overwhelmed by emotion as not to be responsible for his or her actions. This, the new view would argue, is deceptive; emotion is always an act of fully engaged interpretation, of making sense of the world, and therefore we are always legally and morally responsible for what we feel.

This view is also social. Through their emotions people express a full awareness of each other. Through their emotions people attempt to express the moral and human meaning of the institutions in which they live. Yet it is a curious fact of intellectual history that just at the point when cognitive psychology and psychoanalysis are becoming more social in their terms, the discipline of social psychology is unable to receive them.

Until the 19th Century, "social psychology" did not exist as a mode of thought, either in the academies or in society at large. One reason is that social circumstances were not thought to change, fundamentally, the nature of human passions. A single man felt anger, a nation was angry; "anger" in both cases was the same. Similarly, how a person behaved in Athens during the time of Pericles seemed relevant to how a person might act in Paris during the Revolution. If human nature was universal, it was also unchanging. Thus Machiavelli could draw his Prince's attention to all sorts of successes and failures of Roman emperors as instructive lessons for Renaissance statecraft; Bossuet could write a "universal history" of the human race in which the motives of the earliest human beings were the motives Bossuet observed in the people around him every day; Montesquieu moved easily from analyzing greed in an individual to the expression of greed in monarchies, aristocracies, and democracies. The human being was a creature placed in the circumstances of history but not essentially a product of those circumstances.

The historical revolution which began with Vico in the 18th Century, and gathered full force in the 19th Century in the writings of Darwin and Marx, radically altered this view. Biological, economic, and cultural circumstances shape the very nature of a human being, it was thought, and those circumstances accumulate, so that no person, and no age, simply repeats what has come before. The unity of human experience throughout time and space was broken by this view. The only universal principles are the principles of change: they are evolutionary mechanisms or economic forces which create not equilibrium but disruption, growth, and decay.

This historical revolution had its most profound impact in psychology as a whole in ideas of consciousness. In the writings of William James and the young Henri Bergson, consciousness was depicted as a stream, as constantly in motion as time passing. These writers applied to consciousness Heraclitus's famous statement that if you step into a river at two different moments you are not stepping into the same river, and so they began to study the processes of memory, forgetting, and learning in what would now be called developmental terms. Those specifically interested in the psychology of groups were affected by this historizing of human nature in another way.

For them, it was a matter of finding out how as groups develop sentiments arise which have a meaning only in terms of the historical particularities of the group. They wanted to understand sentiments which could not be explained simply in terms of an abstract "human nature." In Tocqueville's second volume of the *Democracy in America,* for example, he analyzed an anxiety and restlessness in America of the Jacksonian era which seemed to him to have no parallel in the past and which was produced by the peculiar circumstances of social equality and weak government in America. In Durkheim's *Suicide,* the pattern and rate of suicides in a society were explained by a weakening of social controls called *anomie;* it would be impossible, Durkheim believed, to understand the fluctuation in suicide rates in a society over time by talking about "despair" in general. Where, when, and under what circumstances explain why despair should be so different in France from despair in America.

Up to the end of the 19th Century, this social analysis of emotion had no name. With the appearance of Gustave Le Bon's *The Crowd* in 1895, it is first called "social psychology." Le Bon's work carried to an extreme the efforts of Tocqueville, Durkheim, and others. He asserted that crowds create types of violent feeling which are wholly different from violent feelings in an individual's life in his family, or under the discipline of army life in a war. Here is his reasoning; it applies to the new discipline as a whole:

> The most striking peculiarity presented by a psychological crowd is the following: Whoever be the individuals that compose it, however like or unlike be their mode of life, their occupations, their character, or their intelligence, the fact that they have been transformed into a crowd puts them in possession of a sort of collective mind which makes them feel, think, and act in a manner quite different from that in which each individual of them would feel, think, and act were he in a state of isolation. There are certain ideas and feelings which do not come into being, or do not transform themselves into acts except in the case of individuals forming a crowd. . . .

> In the aggregate which constitutes a crowd there is in no sort a summing up of or an average struck between its elements. What really takes place is a combination followed by the creation of new characteristics, just as in chemistry certain elements, when brought into contact—bases and acids, for example—combine to form a new body possessing properties quite different from those of the bodies that have served to form it.

The use of chemical imagery here was deliberate. As with his American counterpart George Herbert Mead, Le Bon wanted to understand how emotions were synthesized out of specific social relations.

By the 1920's this way of thinking appeared firmly established and produced a number of significant books of general interest. Sorel had published his *Reflections on Violence,* and there were many followers of Durkheim, notably Maurice Halbwachs, at work in France. In America, Mead and William James had a pronounced effect on John Dewey and his school. In Germany, the thinkers who would come to form the influential "Frankfurt School" of social thought became interested in joining Marxism and psychoanalysis. And then, toward the end of the 1920's, the discipline of social psychology began to come apart.

In the Anglo-Saxon world, the impulse to particularity led to a passion for statistical measurement. The importance of what was being measured became less interesting than the technology for measuring it. As so often happens in the social sciences, what could not be quantified, or what was too complex to be, appeared less real. Of course, triviality was not uniformly accepted for the sake of quantitative certainty. There have been important and far-reaching advances in understanding the relationship between language and society, for instance, but social psychology in the United States and Great Britain has come in the last half-century to have little of import to say about the psychology of power, or collective guilt, or the social organization of fear.

These subjects have remained very much alive in the minds of European writers in this discipline. The difficulty for these continental writers is almost the exact opposite of that of their Anglo-Saxon counterparts. Writing of a social-psychological nature has become more and more a special branch of philosophy. Interviews, case histories, or historical investigations of other sorts rarely appear in their works. They have reacted to the quantifying efforts of the Anglo-Saxons with disdain, but seem to have carried matters a step further and eschewed learning from concrete encounters with other people altogether. Again there are exceptions, but they are not the dominant voices.

Each of these routes leads to the same impasse: there is no sense of human beings as creatures trying to make sense of their lives, as interpreting animals. At its worst, the Anglo-Saxon tradition has been uninterested; at its worst, the continental tradition has no way of knowing. It is a common reproach that one can learn more about the complexity of motives and mutual perception from a reasonably good novel than from a "solid" piece of social-science research; in the domain of social psychology, the reproach unfortunately carries a good deal of truth.

Thus, at a period when other branches of psychology are attempting to include social matters in a more open and complex understanding of how people make sense of their lives, they encounter ideas or procedures in social psychology which are narrower or more deracinated than their own.

This impasse has, in the last few years, come to be widely admitted. There have been a number of attempts to make the discipline of social psychology adequate—intellectually, if not officially and academically—to the expectations other branches of learning have of it. The work of Jurgen Habermas and his colleagues in Germany on patterns of communication is one beginning; serious writers in the women's movement like Jessica Benjamin, Nancy Chodorow, and Juliet Mitchell have connected intimate experience and social life in new ways. Another means to open up this discipline is to enquire into the social organization of emotion itself, and to ask how different kinds of emotions are organized differently in modern society. This is the kind of enquiry which I am pursuing.

Authority, fraternity, solitude, and ritual are four distinctively social emotions. Three of them build bonds to other people; one does not. As expressions of feeling about other people, all these emotions require historical study: which people are we talking about, when, and under what circumstances? It has become an almost automatic reflex of the modern historical imagination, however, to focus on the illnesses of modern society, rather than on its strengths. It does seem to me that the experience of these four emotions is troubled in modern society, and it is an account of these troubles which I wish to give, but I am also convinced that one can see in how these troubles have arisen ways in which they might be eased. That is, I think it is possible from an enquiry into how people now feel authority, fraternity, solitude, and ritual to derive ideas of a more political and visionary sort; it is this connection between social-psychological analysis and political vision which is my aim.

Solitude is an emotion of absence; authority is a bond between people who are unequal; fraternity is a bond built between people who are similar; ritual is a bond built between people who are unified, whether as equals or not. If each of these emotional experiences engages all aspects of the faculties of interpretation—sensation, reflection, logical construction, fantasy—then the axiom Le Bon laid down for social psychology has to be re-examined. His notion was that people felt by virtue of their circumstances: if in a crowd, they felt fraternity as a crowd; if working-class, they felt authority in terms of being workers. The interpretative faculties became prisoners of social circumstances in Le Bon's writings, and subsequently in much social-psychological writings. Is this prison of circumstance really the way people make sense of their lives in society? Of course there is a simple way of answering "no," by carrying Le Bon's position to an extreme. At this extreme, the chemistry of the group is so potent that people are automatons, their understanding and expression blindly determined. In this case there is no interpretation at all; people simply act out a program. Le Bon himself was less extreme, more intelligent. What he did believe was that the chemistry of groups was a force which created sentiments purified of individual variations, and to the extent that a person was caught up in the chemistry of the group, he had lost himself.

But if we imagine the economy and politics of society itself as contradictory rather than uniform, as a house in which confusion and pain are normal rather than the exception, then this view of Le Bon's will not do. The more engaged, committed, and emotionally involved people are in social life, the more dissonances they will of necessity feel. Interpretation of what is happening will be a difficult and demanding activity. The bonds of authority or fraternity will not be like Brancusi sculptures, pure and solid, but rather ambiguous, constantly shifting, varying from person to person. What sort of commonalities exist under these conditions, which are the conditions of real history? What sort of emotional experience is shared? To find some answers to these questions is also the aim of this project.

In order to understand emotional bonds in this way, I have selected as materials for these essays case histories, either from my own work or work published by others, as well as diaries and letters; these I have tried to make speak to more general ideas and theories about authority, fraternity, solitude, and ritual. My purpose in working this way is to show how the process by which a bond like authority is felt into being, and why there are dissonances from person to person in the experience of it. The limitation of this way of working is that it won't tell, for example, how many people are afraid of authority in England at the present moment. What it can do is illuminate what a general social theory about the fear of authority means in concrete human terms, and suggest new ways of thinking matters through.

# I

# Negation

# 1

# The Fear of Authority

*Fatherless now, you must deal with the memory of a father. Often that memory is more potent than the living presence of a father, is an inner voice commanding haranguing, yes-ing and no-ing—a binary code, yes no yes no yes no yes no, governing your every, your slightest movement, mental or physical. At what point do you become yourself? Never, wholly, you are always partly him. That privileged position in your inner ear is his last "perk" and no father has ever passed it by.*

The Dead Father,
*Donald Barthelme*

The need for authority is basic. Children need authorities to guide and reassure them. Adults fulfill an essential part of themselves in being authorities; it is one way of expressing care for others. There is a persistent fear that we will be deprived of this experience. The *Odyssey, King Lear, Buddenbrooks* are all about authority weakening or breaking down. Today there is another fear about authority as well, a fear of authority when it exists. We have come to fear the influence of authority as a threat to our liberties, in the family and in society at large. The very need for authority redoubles this modern fear: will we give up our liberties, become abjectly dependent, because we want so much for someone to take care of us?

There are many ingredients of this modern fear. In part it is a fear of the authorities as seducers. In part it is a fear of the act of seduction, of liberty yielding to security. In part it is a fear of the seduced, of the masses who might be weak-willed.

15

Again, most figures of authority do not arouse much enthusiasm because they do not deserve to. An intelligent person remains sane by rejecting the childish collages of strength and compassion which the authorities present as pictures of themselves. Yet our rejection is not connected to our seeing a better image of authority in the mind's eye. And our need for authority as such remains. Desires for guidance, security, and stability do not disappear when they are unsatisfied.

In this book I want to explore what this modern fear of authority is, who are the authorities inspiring it, and what better images of authority ought be in the mind's eye.

## WHAT IS AUTHORITY?

Everyone has some intuitive idea of what "an authority" is, however difficult the idea is to define. The image of an authority which sticks most in my mind comes from watching the conductor Pierre Monteux rehearse an orchestra over a period of some weeks. Monteux, as anyone who saw him in concert knows, was no charismatic showman. His baton movements were restricted within a box he imagined in front of him, a box about eighteen inches wide and a foot high. The audience saw little of the stickwork going on inside that box, but the orchestra was intensely aware of it. A movement of an inch upward was the sign of a crescendo; a movement of ten inches indicated a massive outpouring of sound. Most of the cueing (the indication of a player's entrance) was done with Monteux's eyes. The French horns, always a difficult group to cue, received signals from a raised eyebrow; for the strings, simply a glance from the conductor was enough.

Monteux had a relaxed, complete control of himself, and that assurance was the cornerstone of his authoritativeness. I do not mean he was dogmatic; he would frequently muse over a passage in silence while the orchestra waited, and he would sometimes change his mind. But his ease at being in control prompted others to think it only natural to yield to him. Indeed, this easy assurance allowed him to exercise effective discipline over the players. Partly, this discipline came from the stickwork itself; you had to concentrate hard on Monteux to get the signals. I remember an impossibly hard polyrhythmic section in Stravinsky's *Rite of Spring* in which the cello section was largely guided by watching Monteux's little finger. But it was also Monteux's presence which forged this discipline.

Some conductors, like Toscanini, create discipline by inspiring terror; he screamed, stamped his foot, even threw his stick at the players. A man possessed of the Truth at each moment, he would brook no falseness from others. To avoid his wrath, you did what he said. Monteux was quite different. "Are you sure, cellos, you would like to be so loud?" or "Such a beautiful passage, oboe, if only it is soft." There was no coercion, no threat; there was simply a man who was trying to help one be better. Better, that is to say, play what he wanted, for he knew. His aura was of one who had achieved an understanding that made it possible for him to judge in the most relaxed way. And this too is an essential ingredient of authority: someone who has strength and uses it to guide others through disciplining them, changing how they act by reference to a higher standard.

I know that on stage Monteux had a kindly and avuncular air. He had it with his musicians as well, but he had something else. His authority inspired fear—not of the Toscanini sort, a different kind of fear. A moment in the slow movement of the Second Piano Concerto of Brahms when the solo cello is hideously out of tune: Monteux stops the orchestra and looks at the cellist in total silence. What makes it awful is, you know he would never have done this to the last cello in the section; you failed to live up to what *you* should be, and he is calling you to account. And this is again an element in what made Monteux an authority: he had the strength to see through you, to refuse what your peers accepted. It made you anxious, and kept you on your toes.

Assurance, superior judgment, the ability to impose discipline, the capacity to inspire fear: these are the qualities of an authority. In 1484, Caxton expressed them succinctly in his salutation to King Richard III in the *Chivalry:* "My most redoubted natural and most dreaded sovereign lord, King Richard." The word "dreaded" has a double meaning. It conveys both fear and awe. An authority, in Caxton's sense, is dreaded.

The difficulty in elaborating this intuitive sense of authority is the idea of strength on which it is based. I have never known a bad or an inept musician who managed to preserve his authority over an orchestra for very long. There are very strong musicians, even geniuses, who are unable to translate their musical strengths into authority over an orchestra; Schumann in his later years is the most striking example. But once we move into the realm of politics, work, or family life, the definitions of strength become much more complex, as does the relation of strength to authority.

Take, for instance, the political synonym for strength: power. Often the words "authority" and "power" are used interchangeably. We do so when we call government officials "the authorities." But often again, authority and power are distinguished, as when we say that a government official lacked the authority to engage in some venture. In English the root of authority is "author"; the connotation is that authority involves something productive. Yet the word "authoritarian" is used to describe a person or system which is repressive.

Or take the idea of strength involved in the fear that authority is breaking down. It is the strength of our generation's values and beliefs; we want them to last, but they don't because our bodies don't. In society as in private life, we want a sense of stability and order, and these benefits a regime possessed of authority is supposed to bring. This desire appears in the monuments of authority in public life: massive churches, shrines, government buildings, all symbols that the ruling order of power will last beyond the generation which now rules and the generation which now obeys. Indeed, one meaning of one Latin word for authority, *auctor,* is that the authority can give guarantees to others about the lasting value of what he does. It is solid. But the social bond is no more timeless than the personal. It is historical, it cannot help but change. The strength those monuments of authority symbolize is a defiance of history, a defiance of time.

Most of all, the idea of strength is complex in ordinary life because of what might be called the element of its integrity. There is no question about the integrity of the musicianship of Toscanini, Monteux, or most other orchestral conductors who are viable authorities to their players. But the integrity of the parent who inspires fear and awe in its children, the politician who inspires dread in its citizens, is very much open to question. For the strengths which give these figures authority may not be used in the service of a higher ideal or of nurturing the subjects, but simply of dominating them. The modern fear of authority is exactly of figures who will use their hold over people to perform the most destructive acts. What sort of strength is it that people perceive in a demagogue or in a destructive parent? It too may be founded on giving an impression of assurance and superior judgement, on the ability to exercise discipline and inspire fear; but how do these impressions flow from a malignant source?

Of authority it may be said in the most general way that it is an attempt to interpret the conditions of power, to give the conditions of control and influence a meaning by defining an image of strength. The quest is for a strength that is solid, guaranteed, stable. At the end of Proust's *Remembrance of Things Past,* this authoritative strength is finally found, in Proust's gazing upon Vermeer's *View of Delft.* The picture is timeless and, as with Monteux at work, there is no question of its integrity. In political and psychological life, the interpretation of power never escapes the ravages of time or the question of integrity. In ordinary life, authority is not a thing. It is an interpretative process which seeks for itself the solidity of a thing. Faith, sin, and despair transformed into stone churches. When we speak of a search for authority, the emphasis should be on the word "search"; we know only too well the kind of illusion in which that search seems to have been fulfilled, the thousand-year Reich or the communist Valhalla which put an end to history. In general, it may be said that we are searching for consolation in authority which time never really permits. This search is frustrating; it makes the very subject of what authority is so difficult to define, so elusive. But as long as we are frustrated, we keep our freedom from those masters of illusion who promise us that history is over, and that the search can come to an end.

To speak of authority as a process of interpreting power is to raise the issue of how much the sentiments of authority lie in the eye of the beholder. In modern social thought there are two schools which hold quite different views on this issue.

One holds that the conditions of power largely determine what the subject will see and feel. Its greatest exponent is the sociologist Max Weber. He is no simple social determinist. Many Marxists at the beginning of this century believed that the powers of the ruling classes automatically translated themselves into images of authority: images of who was strong, who could judge others, principles of discipline and fear. These Marxists, most notably Jules Guesde in France, took it as a self-evident truth that the ideas of the ruling classes are the ruling ideas of an age. People do not think about power; they think what the powerful inculcate them to believe. Weber and many others of his generation were dissatisfied with this view. How could you explain the dawn of critical intelligence if it were true, or how could you explain the fact that as a prelude to revolution the ruling classes often lose faith in themselves? This mechanical idea was in any event bad Marxism, the Italian communist Antonio Gramsci was shortly to point out, for the terms of power in a capitalist society are contradictory, and these contradictions, these dissonances, are what prompt people to think. Weber believed that people think about power in a number of ways, but only certain kinds of thoughts will lead them to conceive of the powerful as authorities, and these thoughts are determined by the kinds of controls the powerful exercise.

The perceptions of authority in power fall, in Weber's writing, into three categories. The first is traditional authority, based on "an established belief in immemorial traditions." It is a perception of societies of hereditary privileges, societies in which the terms of inheritance were set so far back in the past that they make sense only in terms of myths and legends, rather than in terms of practical and immediate life. Not only hereditary aristocracies, but such practices as Jewish and Islamic food prohibitions fall under the scope of traditional authority. Their meaning depends not on the actual pollutedness of pigs or alcohol, but on the fact that once very long ago people rejected them. The sense of authority, of stability, comes from the very length of time this memory has endured; it is what we mean when we speak of a custom as hallowed by tradition. The second category of authority is legal-rational authority, which is "based upon the belief in the legality of rules and on the right of those who occupy posts by virtue of those rules to issue commands." Here the sense lies in what a leader or boss actually does; furthermore, its reasons can be described and applied to anyone who holds that position of power. In a traditional scheme, only the sons of a duke are qualified to become future dukes, degenerate or absurd as they may be; in a legal-rational system, anyone who can fulfill the duties of the office is fit to hold it. The final category is charismatic authority, which "rests upon the uncommon and extraordinary devotion of a group of followers to the sacredness or the heroic force or the exemplariness of an individual and the order revealed or created by him." Weber's model for this kind of authority is Jesus or Mahomet. Traditional ways are overthrown by these prophets; the logic of the existing order is dismissed as false. There is the promise of a new Truth, which is absolute, unshakeable, and solid, but previously unknown. Of all the forms of authority, it could be said, as Weber does of the charismatic type: "What is alone important is how the individual is actually regarded by his subjects."

Weber's approach to authority is that of a follower of the philosopher Kant: human beings can think and feel coherently only in categories. The approach makes sense in terms of the subject of authority, for coherence and order are what people are seeking to wrest from all the complex, contradictory circumstances of power. The approach has been subject to attack on these grounds as well: why just these three categories? Are they mutually exclusive? A priest in the Catholic Church is felt to have charisma, in the sense of a "gift of Grace" whenever he officiates at the Mass. The office of priest is traditional, if not hereditary; its charisma is hallowed by centuries of use. (Weber called such a mixture the "routinization" of charisma, but since the priest's charisma is absolute whenever he officiates, this is not a very satisfactory modification.)

The most important general feature of Weber's approach is that he identifies authority with legitimacy. People will not obey, he believes, those they think are illegitimate. The consequence, to Weber, is that we can always tell when a sense of authority exists in a society: it is when people *voluntarily* obey their rulers. If they have to be coerced, it is because they don't find the rulers legitimate. Authority as a belief in legitimacy, measured by voluntary compliance: this is an approach to authority which has become immensely influential in modern social thought. Perhaps its most eloquent spokesman is an unlikely ally, the Italian writer, who wrote in 1939, in *The Ruling Class*,

> [It is false to say that] political formulas are mere quackeries aptly invented to trick the masses into obedience. . . . The truth is that they answer a real need in man's social nature; and this need, so universally felt, of governing and knowing that one is governed not on the basis of mere material or intellectual force, but on the basis of moral principle, has beyond any doubt a practical and real importance.

At odds with this school are those writers who emphasize the process by which people perceive strength in others, apart from the content of what they perceive. Undoubtedly the great voice here is Freud's and it is a tragic voice. The picture presented to us in his late works like *Moses and Monotheism* and *Civilization and Its Discontents* is of images of authority which are formed in childhood and which persist in adult life. Beneath the adult struggles with power, right, and legitimacy, there remain these archaic images of what strength and power should be, so that as adults we are interpreting not what is but really what once was in our lives, like reading a hidden text with more powerful messages. What happened to us in childhood, Freud believes, is that every action of our parents contributed to our image of their strength. The infant has no standards for judgement, no way of separating itself from the parent; whatever the parent does is potent, and the infant cannot imagine, in its egoistic universe, that the parent does anything which has no effect on itself. Is Mommy depressed? It must be my fault. Is Daddy angry? It must be because of something I have done. When they punish me, I don't understand the reasons, but I must have been bad. Do they love me? Then they must love me absolutely.

The story of maturation Freud tells is a story of rebellion against this conversion process. In no person's life is the conversion process ever erased by adulthood, as though it were a mistake on a tape. At first the child simply competes with the parent of the same sex, Freud thought, a competition with a necessarily ambivalent outcome. The little boy Freud imagines wants to take the place of his father, but does not want to lose his father's love. At later stages, adolescents divorce themselves from obedience to their parents, but nonetheless want the parents to care for them whenever they are in need. An adult, Freud hoped, would come to admit the strength as well as the limits of his parents, but would see the strength on its own terms, as a force which belonged to them, made him, but is now not part of his own.

Freud did not believe that many people would come to make this adult interpretation of strength, or feel it strongly. The masses, he believed, are always in danger of regressing back to earlier phases, where they are at once ravenous for the comforts of a stronger person and in a rage against the very strength they so desire. This is the most emotional component of political discourse for Freud: it is the passion to return, to surrender. It is what authoritarian figures capitalize upon, and this "re-infantilization of the masses" is what Freud believed he was seeing in Europe in the 1930's when he came to write his last works. His vision is, at its most extreme, one in which the moral content of adult controls is like pretext, or like strategic weaponry in a game of psychological chess begun the moment every human being was born.

It was Freud's fear that infantile images of strength would haunt the popular imagination of authority which influenced the more socially minded writers of the "Frankfurt School" of social thought. These writers, beginning with Theodor Adorno and Max Horkheimer, and continuing with their students, such as Herbert Marcuse, Erich Fromm, Walter Benjamin, and more marginally Hannah Arendt, were interested in combining psychoanalysis and sophisticated Marxist social criticism. The great work they published collectively on authority was *Authorität und Familie,* printed in exile in Paris in 1936 and unfortunately never translated into English. The English-speaking reader can gather some of its concerns from a derivative volume directed by Theodor Adorno, *The Authoritarian Personality,* published in America after the Second World War. Here the emphasis was twofold. One was to show exactly what were the psychological mechanisms by which childish images of strength persist into adult life: how memory works, how childish images of a parent are projected on adults by adults, and the like. The other emphasis was on the social conditions which encourage or retard the persistence of these infantile patterns. Like the original volume, *The Authoritarian Personality* sought to be much more historical and specific than was Freud about the ways culture plays a role. In the original volume, Horkheimer spoke, for instance, about how as the controls of the bourgeois *paterfamilias* waned in the 19th Century, the state was expected to step in and serve as a surrogate—a theme recently borrowed by Christopher Lasch in his book *Haven in a Heartless World.* In *The Authoritarian Personality,* Adorno tried to show how anti-Semitic beliefs express the needs of people who felt deprived of strong authority figures in childhood, feel themselves to be weak, and want to find alien figures to blame. "The authoritarian personality" as a concept refers to an intersection between two forces: psychological forces, which lead a person to feel desperately in need of strength, and historical and social forces, which shape how he or she expresses those needs.

There have been so many justified criticisms of the approach of *The Authoritarian Personality* that its value as a pioneering work has often been forgotten. Here is the kind of difficulty one encounters in the book. There is a measure of authoritarian attitudes called the F scale. The actual measure of the attitudes is in the form of questions like "Do you [agree] [disagree] that Jews are dishonest about money?" The results of the test showed that working-class people have much more authoritarian attitudes on the F scale than middle-class people. The difficulty with the results is the form of the questions. Most working-class people when faced with middle-class experts tend to be as cooperative as possible; they fear the authority of the researchers administering the tests and don't want to make trouble. Thus they are predisposed to agree and to assent when asked questions in the above way. It seems to make things go more smoothly. If the questions are asked in a different form, as they subsequently have been, these supposedly working-class authoritarian attitudes disappear.

There are many such problems in this piece of research. Its value, however, lies in the very questions it has provoked. It put in question the assumption that Weber and others had made. What people are willing to believe is not simply a matter of the credibility or legitimacy of the ideas, rules, and persons offered them. It is also a matter of their own need to believe. What they want from an authority is as important as what the authority has to offer. And, the point made more strongly in the work of Max Horkheimer, the very need for authority is shaped by history and culture, as well as by psychological predisposition.

In both these modern approaches to authority, there tends to be a missing dimension: the actual give-and-take between the strong and the weak. These views tend to emphasize the ingredients for making an interpretation. They show us the personal motives or the social conditions involved, but they do not show us how the ingredients are used, how an interpretation is constructed through social exchange. Weber presents an image of a strong man who is likely to arouse the feeling of charisma; the process of arousal is not his concern. The F scale shows us the result of feeling vulnerable and weak and having an alien force in society to blame; the steps leading to this result the scale in itself does not explain.

It is more than a matter of intellectual curiosity which would prompt us to enquire into this missing dimension, this architecture of interpretation. The dilemma of authority in our time, the peculiar fear it inspires, is that *we feel attracted to strong figures we do not believe to be legitimate.* The sheer existence of this attraction is not peculiar to our times; the middle circles of Dante's inferno are populated by those who loved God but followed Satan. But these were sinners who broke the rules of society when they were alive. What is peculiar to our times is that the formally legitimate powers in the dominant institutions inspire a strong sense of illegitimacy among those subject to them. However, these powers also translate into images of human strength: of authorities who are assured, judge as superiors, exert moral discipline, and inspire fear. These authorities draw others into their orbit, like unwilling moths to a flame. Authority without legitimacy, society held together by its very disaffections: this strange situation is something we can make sense of only by understanding how we understand.

This situation would be a contradiction in terms to Weber: how could we want the approval of, and thus willingly submit to, persons we do not believe are legitimate? It would be comprehensible to Freud; it would seem to him a perfectly adolescent experience of authority. But his definition of "legitimacy" would be too narrow. What happens when the dominant images of strength really are illegitimate? When they are malignant, when they in fact lack integrity? It is not irrational under these circumstances to rebel against them. Nor, I believe, is the magnetic attraction they nonetheless exert to be explained alone in terms of infantile, regressive wishes to be controlled. In the very way this illegitimacy is perceived, in the process by which it is articulated, lies also the way a bond is forged with these peculiar masters.

In the first half of this book I shall explore these bonds of illegitimate authority; in the second half I shall explore how more legitimate bonds might come into being. I shall begin the first part of this enquiry by showing how the very act of rejecting authority can be so constructed that a person feels tied to the person he or she is rejecting. The second and third chapters describe two images of authority which are rejected in this way, one an image of authority which proffers a false love, the other an image of authority which proffers no love, no concern for others at all. Both these images of authority are malignant, both are based on illegitimate forms of social control, and both trap those who negate them.

In the second half of the book, the fourth chapter looks at ways people change in intimate life malignant forms of authority which have caused them to suffer. The fifth chapter explores what lessons this intimate experience has for authority in the public realm. The concluding chapter returns to where we began. The churches are testaments in stone to an order, security, and timelessness which never will be, either in politics or intimate life. Is it just illusion which compels us to keep building?

## BONDS OF REJECTION

Most of us have observed marriages in which one partner complains endlessly about the other but never manages to leave. And often what we are hearing is not hatred or disgust which the person is too weak to act upon. Instead there is the need for another person which is not safe to admit, but must be masked, rendered safe by declarations of rejection. Rejection of and a bond to the other person are inseparable.

These bonds of rejection are the way we admit the need for authorities who are not safe to accept. But, unlike a marriage between two supposedly equal adults, the bonds of rejection in authority are based on people with unequal power. The fear in an authority relationship is what the superior would do with that power. Or, at least, this seems the logical reason. But it is also true that people need other people's strength, and sometimes people feel that the actual figures of authority in their lives are not so strong as they should be. The language we find to reject these actual figures may help us define the figures we want, like printing a positive from a photographic negative. But we need the negative to do the printing. A bond is built to people we are rejecting; they are the point of departure. By knowing them, we know what we want.

In modern society we have become adept at building bonds of rejection with authorities. These bonds permit us to depend on those whom we fear, or to use the real to imagine the ideal. The trouble is that these bonds also permit the authorities to use us: they can exercise control of a very basic sort over those who seem on the surface to be rebelling.

I should like to describe three ways these bonds of rejection are built. The first concerns the fear of an authority's strength; it is a bond I shall call "disobedient dependence." The second is printing a positive, ideal image of authority from the negative which exists. The third is built on a fantasy about the disappearance of authority. And I should like to describe these bonds in terms of particular cases. There is a difficulty in doing so. To explain a case history fully is to become ever more particular. My intent is not to give a complete account of what makes these particular people tick, but rather to render the language of bonds of rejection in a concrete form, to make it audible in the lives of actual people. It is a language which in modern society we have become adept at speaking, but often do not realize we speak.

A person who speaks the language of disobedient dependence was aged twenty-five at the time I interviewed her. Helen Bowen* came to a community mental health clinic in Boston one spring because she felt under great tension and wanted a prescription for tranquilizers. Asked if there was some event which had set off the tension in the recent past, she said she had just broken up with her boyfriend. The prescription was given and she left, only to return to the clinic a week later complaining that it was not strong enough. The doctor, checking the use of the pills, found that she had taken only a few at odd intervals, and suggested she enter therapy, a suggestion she accepted. She asked for another therapist, however, because she thought the doctor had given in to her request for pills too quickly, a conviction shared by other staff at the clinic when the doctor described her case.

Her boyfriend was black, as she explained when her therapy began; Helen Bowen herself was from an Irish family. The therapist, trying to pin down the relation between the breakup and her request for pills, found that the separation had in fact occurred three months before; the event which seemed to send her to the clinic was a massive argument with her parents about her relations to men and to themselves, one of many such arguments.

The affair had begun two years before, when Miss Bowen was twenty-three and the young man, a hospital attendant, was twenty-six. After seeing each other for three or four months, the couple decided to live together. The prejudices in Boston against interracial couples made it impossible for them to find an apartment they could afford, she said; only wealthy couples could afford to live in tolerant communities like Cambridge or Newton. She therefore kept her own apartment in a white area of the city, and the man took an apartment on the edge of the Roxbury slums which would be safe enough for a white woman to visit. She visited two to three evenings a week.

The arguments with her parents about this young man arose

*Not her real name; details of her life have also been changed.

because this affair was in time span and arrangement similar to an affair she had with a black student when she was a sophomore in college, aged eighteen. The parents reproached her, she said, for two things. First and obviously, for dating black men; second, for "not being serious," by which they meant she did not live full time with these men, had no desire to marry them or anyone else, and therefore should have chosen more suitable casual partners.

Asked if she talked about race a great deal with either man, she claimed she did not. She was not an "activist," she said, and just happened to fall in love with these two particular human beings. Furthermore, she said, between these two men she had an affair with a healthy, marriageable white man. Asked what her parents had thought about this, she said that they were delighted, but that neither the man nor she wanted to spend much time with her parents, so that the parents barely knew him.

Helen Bowen was born in a middle-class neighborhood outside the Irish ghettos of Boston. Her father worked for the city in a white-collar job and her mother was a substitute teacher in local schools. There were some black children in her neighborhood whose parents were at the top of the black community in the city because they were bureaucrats; her own father was in a car pool with a black man who also worked at City Hall.

Miss Bowen did reasonably well in school, and went on to a local college where she majored in advertising. When she met the first black man she had an affair with, he was undecided between preparing to be a doctor or also following a career in advertising. Their relationship lasted a year and at the end of it he was still undecided. Asked if she tried to help him make a decision, she said she was afraid to get involved in the problem, because it would have been too much of a "responsibility." In fact, she ended the affair because she felt the young man was getting "too dependent" on her.

The second affair with a black man had some parallels to the first. A hospital attendant, he was at twenty-six exploring ways of becoming a paramedic (that is, a person who performs certain medical procedures but is not a registered doctor). He too, she thought, had a dependent character, and she was just as pleased as not that they lived separately. Indeed, when asked if she could have lived in the man's apartment, she said it would have been possible, she supposed, but she really didn't want to spend all her time with one person.

Compared to other people she knew, however, she spent a good deal of time with her parents, frequently spending the weekend at their house "because it's relaxing and I don't have to do anything." The therapist asked what then happened during her affair with the white man, a period when she didn't want to spend time at home. "Oh, they thought this was fine, since it might have meant I was so serious I was going to get married." The question was repeated about why *she* didn't want to spent time at home then; no response.

Another fact about these weekends home soon emerged. Though she described them as relaxed, the subject of her boyfriends was constantly discussed by her parents and herself. Indeed, Miss Bowen seemed to bring up the subject if her parents did not. On it, her parents presented a united front: some things are socially unacceptable and cause too much personal pain, especially if the girl is not willing to marry. Off it, the parents went their separate ways. Miss Bowen remarked that her mother had quite different ideas from her father and no hesitancy in expressing them.

The relations between Miss Bowen and her brother were from childhood close but balanced; two years separated their ages. They shared each other's friends until Miss Bowen was fourteen or fifteen, when she began to date older boys and associate with older girls. It appeared at one session that Miss Bowen was quite oblivious to the possible attitudes of her brother toward her black friends; at later sessions, she remarked that her brother wanted to be friends with them and went out of his way to do so; at yet a later session, she revealed that in fact her brother had taken sides with her latest friend in their separation, and that the two men continued to see each other.

There is something elusive about Miss Bowen's character. She is a likeable person, yet quite aloof. In her work, other people seem to respect her abilities—she writes advertising copy for a medium-size agency—but it is hard to tell if she has made any close friends there. She seems to come alive when talking about her own reactions to the dependency she perceives in other people; on these occasions she gestures with her hands, for instance, while normally she does not.

What caused the massive fight with her parents which sent her to the clinic was her parents' suggestion one weekend that she might, now that she was free of her affair, like to move to another city. They claimed, she said, that the suggestion was wholly "innocent": some fresh experience, new friends, a new scene. Miss Bowen was enraged by the suggestion, but kept silent until her father said that a young woman ought to see something of the world before getting married, and that Helen only knew Boston. Miss Bowen erupted, accusing them of wanting to get rid of her, of not loving her except when she was a "problem" to them. For the first time she can remember, her father in turn became so angry that he left the house, drove away in the car, and did not come back for a couple of hours. Her mother went to her room. Miss Bowen left the house as soon as her father returned, returned to her apartment, and began having the first of a series of tension headaches for which she eventually sought help.

The common-sense interpretation of Miss Bowen's racial experiences would be, I suppose, that she is using these young black men as a weapon in her rebellion against her parents; it would be easy to say that, in the most general terms, she is rebelling against authority. Behind this common-sense interpretation is a sociological assumption. It is that authority can be measured by obedience. In the writings of Max Weber, for example, authority is said to produce voluntary obedience. Sheer obedience tells us nothing, Weber believed, about authority. If Miss Bowen's parents could force her, legally or through controlling her allowance, to give up these black men, all we would know is that they had the power to make her obedient. The moment someone obeys of his or her own volition, however, that person thinks of power as "possessing" authority.

Miss Bowen's actual experience calls into question the equation of the presence of authority with voluntary obedience. Miss Bowen is in thrall to her parents; the decisions she makes about her own erotic life depend first and foremost on her knowledge of whom her parents would approve or disapprove of. What they would like, she negates; she has chosen two men whom she knows they will disapprove of. What they would like is, however, the controlling factor. She is more surely bonded to them than a young person who can make erotic decisions without worrying compulsively about what his or her parents would say. The very act of disobeying, with all its confrontations, anxieties, and conflicts, knits people together. In Miss Bowen's case, it did so physically as well as emotionally. It was during the periods of dating black men that she wanted to spend weekends at home, while when she dated the white man her parents approved of, she had no desire to do so. It is during her periods of disobedience that she lets them take care of her on weekends; defiance erects a barrier which makes her feel safe enough to taste the pleasures of dependence. To say she is rebelling *against* authority is a mistake; she is rebelling "within" authority, guided by a very marked assumption that their desires and their will matter most in the conduct of her own life. She disobeys, but they regulate the terms.

This is disobedient dependence. It is based on a compulsive focusing of attention: what would they want? Once their will is known, a person can proceed to act—against them. But they are the central characters; compulsive disobedience has very little to do with genuine independence or autonomy. The meaning of the term "dependence" in this form of authority also involves a peculiar definition of being close to another person. Miss Bowen's story gives some specific clues about what the terms "dependence" and "closeness" mean when one person negates the will of another. These clues are:

1 She chose black men ambivalent about what to do with their lives.
2 When the men turn to her for help in choosing, she runs away.
3 She shows unusual physical animation, as with the use of her hands, when discussing how dependent men make her feel and the general fear she has of being burdened or invaded by others.

These clues suggest how, in order for Miss Bowen to feel safe in being close to another person, she must erect some insuperable barrier between herself and that person. In the case of the parents, the black men permit her to become once again her parents' daughter, living at home, relaxing with them on weekends; the tense and anxiety-ridden subject of the black men is the way she, however, keeps her parents safely at bay. This relation to her parents is balanced by her relations to the human barriers themselves: *they* must never become dependent on her. If her parents had learned to tolerate blacks, she once told the therapist, "I probably would have found something else."

In Miss Bowen's fear of being openly dependent, a particular use is made of race: it is a symbol of transgression. Transgression is perhaps the most forceful element in the practice of disobedient dependence. It involves something more than saying no. It involves proposing an alternative others cannot accept. A child who simply says "I refuse" is in a far weaker position than a child who says "I want something else"; the subordinate possesses a rationale for the barrier.

In the struggles of disobedient dependence, the world into which a person has entered through the desire to transgress is seldom, however, a real world of its own, a true alternative which blots out the past. In Miss Bowen's life the young black men are not substitutes for her father; they are of use to her as instruments against her father, and this is perhaps why her second black lover once told her, "You are the most racist person I know." This act of negating authority implies that the locus of strength is in the person one must defend against, rather than in an ally one can find by crossing a moral barrier. But this real strength is below the surface, an invisible presence.

Miss Bowen's contacts with the mental health clinic give some clues to what this real strength would look like if it could be seen. The pertinent facts are:

1  Miss Bowen asks for medication and is given it.
2  She complains the medication is not strong enough, but she does not use it as much as is prescribed.
3  She asks for another doctor upon her return to the clinic, complaining that the first doctor gave in too quickly to her demands.

In acting this way, Miss Bowen is asking a question: who is strong enough to take care of me? She is also setting the conditions for a satisfactory answer: it must be someone who is strong enough to oppose me. A detail during the course of therapy exemplifies the question and the conditions she sets for an answer. Recall the moment when the therapist asked Miss Bowen why she didn't visit her parents with her white male friend. When she evaded answering, the therapist repeated the question, and she fell silent. After a while the therapist asked what she was thinking, and she replied she felt "caught," "conquered," "trapped." It was after this session that she began to open up much more to the therapist. He had opposed her, repeating his question, refusing her evasion.

The conviction which arose in Miss Bowen's mind was similarly that if her father would challenge her about the blacks, then he must be really strong—but strong in ways she couldn't see. And these reserves of strength she imagined in him focused her attention upon him much more than upon her mother, who was not as challenging to her. When her father finally refused to play the game of opposition any more, she didn't feel relieved, therefore, but instead felt her life had cracked apart. It was at this point she went in search of a therapy. He had broken the bond.

What is missing to explain Miss Bowen's language of disobedient dependence are those elements in her parents' life she fears. This enquiry would take us further into the particulars of her father's personality, her mother's, and their parents' in turn. What is socially significant about this relationship is the social bond which has been created on the basis of these fears: a covenant in which dependence and transgression are inseparable.

Rejection can be organized in a somewhat different way, so that the figure in authority is denied directly, rather than by use of a third, symbolic party like Miss Bowen's blacks. This more direct rejection appears in the language of idealized substitution. And this language, too, tightens the knot between the actual figures of authority and their unhappy subjects. The example I shall cite comes from a period of four months I spent observing accountants in a large industrial concern. There were sixteen accountants, three assistant heads-of-section, and one head-of-section in this department. The office was not oppressive; the accountants did not have to be threatened by the assistant heads or the head-of-section. There was a lot of work to be done, and they did it, often staying after hours to clean up their desks. At the same time, the relations between superiors and subordinates were tense and troubled.

Although the accountants believed in the value of the actual work they did, they had contempt for the head-of-section, and for two of her three assistants. "She spends all her time doing politicking and infighting," one accountant said. "I asked her about how to enter something, and she said 'Just use your best judgement,' which means either she doesn't care or she doesn't know about it." Another accountant remarked, "We had a meeting with the assistant heads to figure out a better system of journal entries for a client, and all they could talk about is what will she [the head] think." One assistant head, who is liked, commands respect from the accountants "because she knows how to divide up the work, and seems concerned about her own quality"; but she is also criticized for "not being a real leader." When asked what the term "a real leader" meant, the accountants responded as follows: "Someone who really drives you, who gets more out of you than you think you've got in you." "Someone who is willing to be a bitch for the sake of doing a first-class job." "Someone who says, 'Lookit, girls, if I knock myself out, you knock yourself out to do it.' " In other words, a real leader gets respect by being coercive and punitive—not exactly what Weber had in mind.

It could be said, of course, that in this office there is a split between functional authority and personal authority; the accountants willingly do the work, but not because they believe in the bosses as exemplary figures. The trouble is that the process of working is colored by the way the bosses are perceived. When the head-of-section asks someone to do a task near lunchtime, for instance, the person that day often takes an especially long lunch hour; it is just the day he or she had to do some shopping. The work is started late and often finished after hours, when the bosses are not there. There was a disastrous Christmas party in which one accountant, after too many cups of rum-and-vodka punch, came up to one of the assistant heads and started in on a long recital of her personal defects before he was pulled away by the other accountants. Since absenteeism is rife in the office, overall productivity is low, although when the accountants are actually on the job they work hard. Erratic, tense, contemptuous of their superiors, they take pride in doing their jobs well but are little concerned about the rate of productive output. "That's the bosses' problem"—yet the boss is thought illegitimate because she spends so much time in bureaucratic infighting defending her operation.

One morning I interviewed the head-of-section just after she had decided to move an employee who did not have the necessary skills to stay in her particular department. As is usual in large corporations, such personnel decisions are formally taken by committee. "This protects me from the employees feeling it is a personal and arbitrary decision on my part," the head-of-section explained. She could not have been more mistaken. "That woman is afraid to stand up and say what she thinks," an accountant told me when the decision became known. "She is always hiding behind the personnel committee."

In one way, these accountants deal with their boss the way Miss Bowen does with her father. They erect a barrier through their erratic attendance at work, which defies the boss. But their attitudes about the boss are rather more explicit than Miss Bowen's attitudes about her father. They use the boss as a negative model; whatever she is and she does, the opposite is what they want. This is the process of idealized substitution: a real, creditable authority is the opposite of whatever you are.

In this way, the subjects come to depend on the person in charge. That person serves as a point of reference. For instance, nearly half of the accountants had transferred into this section from another where they felt the work was too regimented. When I asked those who had transferred about this, they became defensive. Why shouldn't they work in an easier section, many of them replied. And when it was pointed out that they were complaining about a boss who did not regiment them, and so made their work easy, they would reply that "this is a different matter," or "she's something else again." Asked if any of them would consider transferring again, all of them replied that they would not. One assistant head-of-section had a rather clear notion of what was going on. "They need her," she said; "they don't like her and they're not lazy, but they need her to give the work a point."

The fear which operates in idealized substitution is a fear of being cut loose, of having no moorings, no point of reference to say why one is working, serving, or dependent. If the master is bad, weak, then an image appears of what is good. To print this positive, it is often necessary to exaggerate the defects of the actual superior, to give the superior a kind of "negative potency." This inflation is what those in control pick up on. In the accountants' office, the boss resented her employees for being so "disrespectful." But also, because she felt they were "exaggerators," not really "responsible," she felt superior to them. They felt she was a weak flunky, she felt they were childish and unrealistic, and these negatives locked them into each other's lives. Is she an authority figure to them? It depends what the term means. She is not a role-model for them, but without her presence they could not imagine one. And the sense they make of her leads to define how, in her own mind, they are weak.

A third way the bond between masters and servants can be built beneath the surface of rejections is through the fantasy of disappearance. Everything would be all right if only the people in charge would disappear. Here is a primitive instance of the fantasy, in a speech made at a rally of Youth Against War and Fascism, a radical group in New York, some years ago:

> You know what capitalism is? Capitalism is a cancer. You know what you do with cancer? You cut it out. Don't play with it, don't treat it nice and hope it will be better. You cut it out. Capitalism makes people unhappy. That's all you need to know. Cut it out, be happy, what are you waiting for? . . .

The thinking is so stupid as to be beneath notice—save for the last sentence: "Cut it out, be happy, what are you waiting for?" Anyone who took this speech seriously would be willing to wait forever. Everything which exists now depends on this evil force; if it disappeared, what in fact would remain?

A more complicated picture of fantasies of disappearance, and their immobilizing consequences, is presented by Alexander Mitscherlich's *Society Without the Father,* as in the outlines of the following case history:

> . . . A student aged thirty-five had twice failed in his examinations. He was severely inhibited and unable to concentrate either on his work or on any other aim in life. His father was an official who had suffered throughout his life from the fact that he had not taken his matriculation examination; he spent his working life among colleagues and seniors who enjoyed that distinction. In spite of their

bad performance at school, the patient and his brother were forced by their father to sit for their matriculation. Their mother's horizon was narrowed by obsessional neurosis, and she had grown depressive under her husband's resentment-laden tyranny. When he came home in the evening she filled his ears with tales of the boys' misdeeds during the day, and the result would be a paternal punitive expedition to their room. And so it went on. The boys lived in perpetual terror of their mother's denunciations and their father's severity. . . . The stronger the paternal pressure, the more insuperable was the inhibition on learning. . . . Despite his natural ability, [the patient] put up a total resistance, based on his unconscious introjects and his defence against them, to all systematic and logically coherent knowledge. His inability to work was his only way of simultaneously avenging himself on his father and punishing himself for doing so. . . .

One strategic purpose of such resistances, as Freud was the first to point out, is the subject's belief that if failure is stubborn enough, eventually the pressure on the subject will disappear. The trouble is that if the pressure does disappear, the subject feels absolutely bereft: he or she was not even good enough for anyone to care about. There is a need to fantasize that everything would be all right if only the authority figure didn't make his presence felt, and a fear that without that presence there would be nothing. The authority figure is feared, but even more the subject fears he will go away. The result of this process is that language of contingency in which everything wrong is the fault of the presence of an authority, and it matters desperately that the authority be present.

The social saliency of these bonds of rejection is the ease with which we build them; is how natural it now seems to speak the language of disobedient dependence, idealized substitution, or fantasized disappearance. The reasons this language of authority is so easy to speak are rather deeply embedded in the past. Commonly, those who do attitude surveys—and find how striking is the amount of disaffection and rejection of authority among the people they survey—explain the results in terms of recent causes: Watergate in America, the end of the postwar miracle in Western Europe, the advent of affluence and the new "spoiled classes" in Russia and parts of Eastern Europe. Of course these immediate factors contribute to what we immediately see. But the language of rejecting authority goes back to a noble aim at the end of the 18th Century: instilling the desire for liberty among the masses of the people. And the bonds of rejection which this paradoxically creates were first forged as the language was extended from politics in the 18th Century to economic conditions in the 19th Century.

## THE FAITH OF THE NEGATIVE SPIRIT

One of the deepest marks the French Revolution made on modern thinking was to convince us that we must destroy the legitimacy of rulers in order to change their power. Destroy faith in them, then we can destroy their regimes. And if there was a single event which bore witness to this belief, it was the killing of Louis XVI in 1793. He was not killed because as a person he was a threat to the dawning new order: a passive and ineffectual ruler, he impressed his brother-in-law Joseph II of Austria and many others as stupid, weak, and without any redeeming arrogance. But the majesty of his office was a threat; the aura of authority of the King, as long as there was a King, inhibited the revolutionaries from changing fundamental structures in the society. The urban masses felt inhibited; more interestingly, their leaders felt inhibited. And so the personal nonentity who was King was beheaded. In reflecting on this event, the Englishman Edmund Burke made an interesting comparison to the beheading of Charles I by the Puritans 144 years before. In both cases, the King was formally put to death in the name of a higher principle, the Puritans' God, the Revolution's People. But the balance of weights was very different. In the French Revolution it was the sheer act of killing the King which was so important; this act of destroying his aura of legitimacy is what would set the people free.

By negating the legitimacy of the ruler, we begin to set

ourselves free: this faith is the Revolution's legacy. The first heirs received it in the purest form. Here for example is a purple passage from a tract on the French Revolution which the young German philosopher Fichte published in 1793:

> From the moment we are born, reason has asked us to engage in a long and terrible duel between liberty and slavery. If you are stronger, reason told us, I will be your slave. I will be a very useful servant for you; but I will always be a restless servant, and as soon as there is some slack in my yoke I will defeat my master and conqueror. And once I throw you down, I will insult you, dishonor you, trample you under. Since you can be of no use to me, I will profit by my right of conquest to seek your total destruction.

By the last years of the 18th Century, this faith was no longer directly attached to belief in the Revolution. The people had consumed themselves during the Terror, destroyed their chances of liberty by setting up a new authority—themselves, embodied in the abstraction The People—in place of the old. In 1797, the young Hegel wrote

> ... the distinction is not to be made between [someone who is free and someone who is a slave]. Rather, the first is dominated from without, while the other, having his master within, is by that token his own slave.

Domination, in other words, is everywhere. Those who lead revolutions are as much masters as those who defend Church and King. Freedom comes from pushing out the "master within," whatever his claims. By disbelieving in his legitimacy, you drive him out; at least your mind is free. And what Hegel put in philosophic terms was expressed in more popular forms throughout Germany, Austria, and Italy with the advent of Napoleon. Don't believe in him and "his destiny," newspapers in Central Europe exhorted their readers. The moment you believe in his charismatic destiny you will lose the will to fight; if you steadfastly refuse to credit him, even if he conquers our territories, he will not have conquered us. These exhortations Napoleon understood. It was why subversive thoughts about "the legitimacy of the Emperor" ranked high as acts of treason.

It was at the end of the old regime, then, that people began to think that if you destroy legitimacy, you destroy the force of authority. The thinking of Max Weber derives from this heritage. But the heritage has a broader scope than what he made of it. Freedom is an essential part of it, and freedom is a matter which rarely appears in his writing. To disbelieve is to be free—free in spirit, if not in fact.

During the course of the 19th Century, this negating spirit expanded its field from politics to the economy. It became a weapon by which people sought to defend themselves against the forces of market and industrial growth which were transforming European and North American society. These captains of finance and manufacturers made claims which seemed to Tories and socialists alike to be pernicious. Twelve hours a day of labor for a child in the mines was explained as a benefit to society and ultimately to the child (assuming it lived); the market was distributing the resources of the labor market to all. The destruction of the agricultural economy was a similar benefit to society; the dispossessed laborers were now "free" to sell their labor on the open market for the highest price. It seemed to Disraeli no less than to Marx a terrible danger if the people suffering from the new industrial order would come to believe these things; then the mind as well as the body would be enslaved.

We could never make sense of the moral force of this new industrial order, or of the way the bonds of authority gradually separated from the sense of legitimate authority, if we think of the market ideology as alone the principle on which the new rulers justified themselves. The market idea, as Adam Smith proudly announced, banishes the authority of persons; it is a system of exchange which is legitimate only as a system. The closest we come to an image of control, reassurance, or guidance is the "invisible hand" which assures fairness. But the invisible hand is also an abstraction; it is attached to the body of no single human being.

What the market ideology and the market in operation did was to drive a tremendous cleft in society. The market disturbed both the desire for community and the desire for individual liberty. The desire for community expressed itself most obviously in the national movements which gathered force in the last century. Nations wanted to be in control of their destinies, economically as well as politically. The market economy was, however, an international system; prices rose and fell, booms and depressions appeared, beyond the power of any one nation in this system to control. In England and America, moreover, the political control over corporations which existed in the 18th Century was destroyed in the name of free market operations. The market ideology promised the consummation of individual freedom of action. The market in practice was anti-individualistic. It displaced masses of peasants from their land, whatever their own desires to remain. At the moments when the supply of labor in cities exceeded the demand for labor, there was in fact no labor market. If an employee did not like the wages an employer paid, he could go starve; there were plenty of others to take his place. There are many ways in which the conflict between the community and the individual predates the era of high capitalism: in the realm of legal rights for prisoners, for instance, it goes back to the work of Cesare Beccaria in the middle of the 18th Century; in the realm of rights of conscience in religion it goes back to the struggles of the Reformation. The market system of the last century, rather, made the concepts of community and individual ambivalent, and ambivalent in a peculiar way. No specific human being, no human agent, could be held accountable for disturbances in these realms.

The attempt to find someone responsible, to establish images of human strength and control more concrete than the "invisible hand," was the work of authority in the 19th Century. In the economic domain itself, there were attempts to create a sense of community through the boss serving *in loco parentis* to his workers, in company towns most notably, but also as a *patron* in more diverse industrial cities like Lyon,

Pittsburgh, or Sheffield. This authority is a paternalistic figure. There were also attempts to enshrine individualism itself, so that the expert—the engineer, doctor, or scientist with modern technological skills—working alone according only to the dictates of his expertise, yet controlling others, became a figure of authority. Tocqueville calls "the independent ones" the only people of his time securely able to command respect from others and make them afraid. These two figures of authority, who are the subject of the two following chapters, were not extensions of the market ideology. They were figures of strength who were to compensate for its disruptions, resolve its ambiguities. However, the *patron* would take care of his workers only if they would be docile and not pressure him. The autonomous expert would doctor, engineer, or plan cities for other people—yet the conditions of entry into these professions became more and more restricted, so that the need for services always outstripped the supply. The market shaped the appearance of these figures of strength, even as they gave the appearance of rising above it.

Their subjects did not escape the market at all. They continued to be hired and fired according to their employers' needs; they continued to buy services at the highest market rate. The authorities promised protection or aid, but often did not make good on the promises. And from this gap arose the essential feature of modern authority: figures of strength arousing feelings of dependence, fear, and awe—yet the pervasive feeling that there was something false and illegitimate about the result. The personal strength of the authorities was accepted, the value of their strength to others doubted. Here the split between authority and legitimacy began.

A story told of Andrew Carnegie illustrates the process. A reporter went to a city where Carnegie had endowed one of his libraries for workingmen. The reporter fell into conversation with a worker coming out of the library. Asked what he thought about the benefactor, the worker replied, "Mr. Carnegie is a great man, a friend of the common man." They then began to talk of labor troubles in the town, of an abortive strike, and of falling wages. The laborer concluded the interview by saying, "Mr. Carnegie is a great man but this"—gesturing toward the library—"is a fraud." It is a statement in which both the feelings about Carnegie and about his benefactions are equally sincere.

If we experienced power in a cool and distant manner, we could expect a certain consequence from this split. Marx expected it: the perception of illegitimacy would eventually erode the strength seen in an authority. The negative spirit would triumph, the servants would rise up against their masters in whom they no longer believed, and society would be free. But this assumes that feeling the strength of another person, no matter how unjustified you think it, doesn't rebound on you.

The rebound in modern society has been that people feel ashamed about being weak. They use the tools of negation to ward off these feelings of shame, and to defend themselves against the impact of strong people who seem malign. The subjects defend themselves by declaring the illegitimacy of the masters. The language of rejection in the case histories we reviewed shows the final stage of this process: making it safe to declare the need for stronger people, for an anchor in the world, by rejecting the legitimacy of those who are strong. One can then be dependent without being vulnerable.

The cornerstone of this complex process is the feeling of shame about being weaker than, and dependent upon, someone else. In aristocratic or other traditional societies, weakness was not *per se* a shameful fact. One inherited one's weakness in society; it was not of one's own making. The master inherited his strengths; they too were impersonal. Thus in documents of the old regime we often find the plainest speaking of servants to their masters. Man and position were distinct. As Louis Dumont remarks in a study of hierarchy in Indian society, *Homo Hierarchicus,* it is not under these conditions humiliating to be dependent.

In industrial society it became so. The market made positions of dependence unstable. You could rise, you could fall.

The most powerful impact ideologically of this instability was that people began to feel personally responsible for their place in the world; they viewed their success or failure in struggling for existence as a matter of personal strength or weakness. "Poverty," the 19th Century popular writer Samuel Smiles once remarked, "is the portion of those not strong enough to provide for themselves." A number of studies have shown that throughout the 19th and the early 20th Century, down to the Great Depression, people who were caught up in the economic turmoil knew in the abstract that they were in the grip of impersonal forces they could not control; still they took their misfortunes as signs that they had not been strong enough to cope. The notion of survival of the fittest—the credo of Social Darwinism—is entrenched in reverse. If you experience misfortune you are personally responsible for being weak.

Shame about being dependent is the legacy of 19th Century industrial society to our own. The theme is a familiar one in the United States. It began with the countryman's horror of "the indecent servitude of manufacturing"; it persists in a welfare economy, even after a floor has been put on the worst economic disasters and some material guarantees to the dependent are made by law. Studies of poor, urban American blacks, for instance, testify to their belief that to be on welfare, to be dependent upon people who are judging your weakness in order to decide how much you need, is an intensely humiliating experience. For all that these blacks know that the deck may be stacked against them, the internalizing of dependence as shame occurs. There is evidence, again, that similar feelings are experienced by French and English workers on unemployment relief.

These feelings are not "neurotic" or "irrational." They are rather signs of how the phenomenon of dependence has come to stand in our minds as a threatening situation, one in which we are vulnerable and without protection. Novels in the genre of "negative utopias"—like Zamyatin's *We*, Huxley's *Brave New World*, Orwell's *1984*—are parables of how social dependence opens up the possibility of absolute personal debasement for all classes. When Winston, the protagonist of *1984*, has finally surrendered all his own judgement, has become the docile, weak servant of the state, Orwell closes the novel with these words: "He had won the victory over himself. He loved Big Brother." The fear that dependence is debasing began with the material conditions of an unstable market economy; it persists as a fear about the quality of relations between the strong and the weak in the welfare state.

To combat these ambivalences about dependence, this sense of being personally vulnerable when one is dependent, the terms of negating authority have been deployed. They have become defenses against feeling exposed. The fear of dependence is counteracted by doing something more complicated than debating the masters. It is accomplished by calling the integrity of their very person into question. This is how we seek to expunge the "master within." Another person is not legitimate to make demands upon us; if we can come to believe that, then we have a weapon against his making us feel weak or ashamed.

Miss Bowen, the accountants, and Mitscherlich's patient, all of whom speak this language of negation so fluently, show us its terrible paradox. The safety it brings also tightens the knot with the masters. They become necessary objects of fear. Rather than masters driven out from within, they become more firmly rooted within. There is alienation from them, but no freedom from them.

What we need to understand about the larger social dimensions of this bond is the strengths which have come to be seen in the dominant figures of authority, the paternalistic and autonomous figures. What kind of shame has their strength elicited among those who are dependent upon them? What acts of negation have tightened the knot between the two sides?

The deformation of the negating spirit has, perhaps, best been expressed by those who have charted its rise and fall in modern literature. In *Beyond Culture,* Lionel Trilling defined the spirit of negation in the following way:

> Any historian of the literature of the modern age will take virtually for granted the adversary intention, the actually subversive intention, that characterizes modern writing—he will perceive its clear purpose of detaching the reader from the habits of thought and feeling that the larger culture imposes, of giving him a ground and a vantage point from which to judge and condemn, and perhaps revise, the culture that has produced him.

A culture the writer needs to reject, a culture worth rejecting —but a culture the writer needs. It is the point of departure, the anchor, everything is asserted in reaction to it. This produces dependence. Irving Howe remarks: "Modernism consists in a revolt against the prevalent style, an unyielding rage against the official order . . . [but] modernism must always struggle but never quite triumph, and then, after a time, must struggle in order not to triumph." The echoes of this paradox are what we hear in everyday life in the experiences of disobedient dependence, idealized substitution, and fantasies of disappearance. Rejection and need become inseparable. The liberating ends envisioned in the birth of the modern spirit of negation during the first years of the French Revolution are defeated.

This dead end has been characterized in stark terms by Octavio Paz. Negation is for him creatively barren:

> Today . . . modern art is beginning to lose its powers of negation. For some years now its rejections have been ritual repetitions: rebellion has turned into procedure, criticism into rhetoric, transgression into ceremony. *Negation is no longer creative.* I am not saying that we are living the end of art: we are living the end of modern art. [Italics R.S.]

But what then should succeed it? A surrender to the dominant institutions? Withdrawal into the mystic recesses of the self? Resolute hedonism? The trouble is that neither the pains of society nor the need for other human beings would go away.

# 2

# Paternalism, an Authority of False Love

The era of high capitalism destroyed in order to build. The growth rate of cities in the 19th Century, for example, was unprecedented, as was their sheer size. For this growth to occur, the countryside was drained of its population; villages were deserted, the land not tilled. But the destruction of the old order did not mean it was forgotten. Quite the opposite. It was idealized, tarted up, made the subject for regret. The idiocy and harshness of rural life were put out of mind, and the countryside became a place of pastoral ease in which deep and open human relationships seemed once to have existed.

Everywhere in the 19th Century the fragments of the old life which capitalism was shattering were being picked up and treasured as objects all the more precious because they were so vulnerable, too delicate and sensitive to survive the onslaught of material progress. Just as the village was idealized as a community, the stable family, with the younger generations taking their places in the order custom dictated, was idealized as the seat of virtue. To the extent this stable family existed, its suffocations of the young or the lively, which in differing ways Rousseau and Goethe conveyed so powerfully to the previous century, were put out of mind.

The citizen was offered pastiche as a landscape of authority. Images of a broken world were pasted upon a canvas, tinted, and then presented as what trust, security protection, safety ought to be. Forming a community; belonging to one another —this social need was met with "It once existed; we used to." To retain a sense of reality, the citizen had to penetrate the haze of regret, to decompose that landscape, like a painter dissatisfied with a collage who removes step by step what has been pasted together.

Foremost among the pastiche pictures of authority in the 19th Century was the image of a father, a father from a more kindly and stable time, superimposed on the image of a boss. This picture of authority is paternalism, as high capitalism constructed it. Whereas in the 17th and 18th Centuries most fathers were in fact the bosses of their children, in farms or businesses run as family enterprises, in the more fragmented and unstable family conditions of the 19th Century the statement "The boss is a father" was a metaphor. This paternalistic metaphor was frequently and widely used in the new economy, pasted over the stark material fact that bosses were anything but supportive, protective, loving leaders of their employees. And what is interesting about this paternalism, apart from the sheer frequency with which it appeared, is how those subjected to it learned to disbelieve in the pastiche they were offered to view. For they came not only to take apart this particular metaphor; they came to distrust any meaning for power expressed in metaphors. And that distrust of the work of imagination in politics is one of the principal legacies of negation from the 19th Century to our own.

## THE EVOLUTION OF PATERNALISM

Paternalism is often used indiscriminately as a synonym for patriarchy or patrimonialism, an error which comes from assuming that all forms of male domination are basically the same. There are in fact important structural and historical differences in the meaning of these words.

A patriarchy is a society in which all people are *consciously* related by blood ties. Each person defines his or her relationship to anyone else in the society in terms of lineage: "He is the uncle of my second cousin's brother" or "He belongs to the family made by the daughter of my niece's third cousin by her marriage to my father's uncle twice-removed." In a patriarchy, males are the linchpins of these family relationships. They decide who marries whom, property passes through male lines, and so on. In a matriarchy, females are the linchpins. In a polyarchy, neither sex is dominant, but all social relations are still conceived in terms of family ties. The most familiar examples of patriarchy are Old Testament families; the most celebrated, if largely mythical, example of matriarchy are the Brazilian Amazons; and the striking examples of polyarchy are the actual tribes of the Brazilian Amazon described by Claude Lévi-Strauss.

A patrimonial society is like the patriarchal in one way, unlike it in another. Property passes from generation to generation through male relatives; for instance, primogeniture in England and France passed property from eldest male in one generation to eldest male in the next. It is considered legitimate for the male heads of household to determine the marriages of the people in that household. Patrimonialism is different from patriarchy in that people do not conceive of their social relationships exclusively in terms of family. They may think of themselves as "belonging" to a medieval seigneur even though they are not related to him. The male bloodline has become a model for the inheritance of property and position in a society which consciously recognizes there to be ties beside family which knit people together.

A medieval manor is the most obvious example of a patrimonial society, but not the most interesting one. Modern Japan is. Until a few years ago, the patterns of deference and age-grading which ruled the Japanese family were expected to rule in industry as well. Often the younger generation inherited the position of its elders in shops, factories, and corporations, at all levels of the hierarchy. Although these patterns are now beginning to become diffuse, the male bloodline was indeed the principle for the inheritance both of property and position; even when males of different generations were in fact not related by blood, they acted as though they were. As Ronald Dore has pointed out in a comparative study of industrial life in Japan and Britain, the patrimonial model was in no way a brake on Japanese industrial growth. In fact, patrimonialism gave the society a coherence and discipline which may be one of the principal causes Japanese industry grew fast and efficiently.

Paternalism differs from patrimonialism in the most basic way: the patrimony itself does not exist. Property no longer passes legally from father to eldest son according to the principle of primogeniture. Nor does society legally guarantee that the position held by a person in one generation will be held by a relative in the next. For instance, when the intendant system was first set up in France, each of the provinces was to be ruled by an employee of the King rather than by local princes; it was thought in the beginning that the intendancy would pass from father to son, just as positions on the medieval estates of the princes had earlier done. This would be patrimonialism. Gradually the intendancies were offered for sale when one came vacant, and eventually they were offered—a shocking idea at the time—to the person who through connections or sheer ability was thought best able to administer the province. This was the end of patrimonialism. In technical terms, what began as a status ended as an office. Without something stable to inherit—without statuses, fixed property, dowries—patrimonialism falters.

In a paternalistic society, males continue to dominate. The domination is based on their roles as fathers: protectors, stern judges, the strong. But this basis is symbolic rather than material as in a patrimonial order. In a paternalistic society no father can guarantee to his children a known place in the world; he can only act protectively.

In one way, paternalism may seem the only form of male dominance possible in a society of great change like that of the 19th Century. The material organization of life was in so much flux that a man was in danger who based his claims to power on his ability to pass on a fixed amount of property to someone else in thirty or forty years. If a male were to legitimate his power, he would have to do so in terms of symbols and beliefs cut loose from such material tests. The Japanese example is a warning against thinking paternalism the only form of male dominance suited to the rapid development of capitalism. And it is also true that in modern capitalism families of the rich and poor tend in general to reproduce their social conditions; the son of a corporation president has a much better chance of going to Eton, joining the right clubs, and becoming a corporate president himself than does the son of a plumber. But this is only in general; no particular father can employ the law to give a guarantee. Paternalism is male domination without a contract.

The result is to introduce a certain ambiguity about the authority figure. What a child learns about its father's protectiveness is not what a young adult will learn about a boss. Work is not a natural extension of family. The authority figure cannot be explained by the mirror assumption"; that is, the assumption frequently made by psychoanalysts that larger social relationships mirror the primary erotic, aggressive, or adjustive relationships within the family. At best, as every human being passes out of the family into which he or she was born, that human being sees these relationships reflected in work or politics as in a distorting mirror. Moreover, what does it mean for a man in power to say to another adult "Trust me," and have that appeal awaken archaic memories of the trust one experienced as a child? True, a connection in memory between a father and a boss may strengthen the hold of that boss over the discipline and obedience of his employees, but what is the substance of this symbolic connection? It certainly is not, as in a patriarchy, that all society is a family; nor is it, as in a patrimonial order, based on a material and contractual idea of fathering itself.

The first signs that patrimonialism was weakening appeared long before the advent of industrial capitalism. These first signs were greeted by many as a great advance forward in human liberty.

The withering of patrimonialism appeared to John Locke, for instance, as the way to curb the power of kings. The king would not be able to base his powers on the rights of family inheritance. He would have to justify his actions by whether or not they were rational. Once family and state were separated, it would no longer be possible for a leader to say, as Nicholas I did, "Do not question me! Know that I am your father; that is enough!" Locke's great writings on this subject are his *Two Treatises on Government* (1690). Both treatises are an attack on Sir Robert Filmer, who pushed to an extreme the patrimonial argument that authority in the family and in the state are identical. Locke's argument is divided into two parts. The first concerns the nature of power itself; he writes in the second section of the *Second Treatise:*

I think it may not be amiss, to set down what I take to be Political Power. That the Power of a Magistrate over a Subject may be distinguished from that of a Father over his Children, a Master over his Servant, a Husband over his Wife, and a Lord over his Slave. All which distinct Powers happening sometimes together in the same Man, if he be considered under these different relations, it may help us to distinguish these Powers one from another. . . .

The second half of his argument concerns the relationship between authoritative power, by which he means just power, and freedom. Again from the *Second Treatise:*

> Thus we are born Free, as we are born Rational; not that we have actually the Exercise of either: Age that brings one brings with it the other too. . . . The Freedom of a Man at years of discretion, and the Subjection of a Child to his Parents, whilst yet short of that Age, are so consistent, and so distinguishable, that the most blinded Contenders for Monarchy, by Right of Fatherhood, cannot miss this difference, the most obstinate cannot but allow their consistency.

The consequences of Locke's doctrines were radical, as he knew and as their immense influence attests. It would no longer be possible to speak of "freedom" as a universal principle; freedom in the family differs from freedom in the state. Casting off the yoke of the family as an image of the political order would also, Locke realized, mean losing a sense of continuity. In every human life an immense divide ought to open up when a person becomes adult; experiences from childhood won't count as guides to rational adult action.

In the early phases of capitalism, Locke's ideas were realized in the most concrete ways. Large segments of the state bureaucracy in England and France became bureaucratic offices in the modern sense rather than inheritable statuses. The great divide in the life cycle was realized through the increasing separation of household and workplace. Whereas the medieval pattern was for craft and commercial labor to be physically located in the house, and the father to serve as the boss of the rest of the family, in the later 18th Century the rapidly growing enterprises moved to large quarters where many people unrelated to each other worked together and where people began to labor as individuals rather than as part of family units. The divide also opened up in the lives of the masses of people who were agricultural laborers. The enclosure of land created vast numbers of migrant workers, sharecroppers, and tenant laborers, and they too tended to work as individuals rather than as part of family units. In France, where the mass of peasants rented land, every increase in taxation was a motive for the young to leave the plots of their parents and move to another commune or even another province where they might start out more cheaply for themselves. All these material changes drained the reality out of a patrimony, and so out of patrimonialism.

No social order, of course, goes out like a light. As late as 1952, a study of women in Germany found that 62 percent brought a legally determined dowry to their marriages. In parts of Southern Italy today, *padrones* are not only bosses of agricultural workers but often the heads of family clans to which those workers belong. In a deeper way, fathers continued to control the power and life chances of their children throughout the Victorian era. Steven Thernstrom, in a study of working-class families in 19th Century America, concluded that fathers often sacrificed the occupational chances of their sons, sending them to work at an early age rather than letting them continue at school and so get training for better jobs; the fathers did so because they wanted to amass money as quickly as possible in the family in order to buy a house or other property.

The main problem with Locke's theory, however, was his belief that once the material foundations of patrimonialism were destroyed, liberty for adults outside the family would increase. What he and other liberal idealists did not anticipate is that what could be materially destroyed could be imaginatively rebuilt: metaphors linking fathers and bosses, fathers and leaders. Paternalism attempted to accomplish by a new means what patrimonialism had accomplished: a legitimation of power outside the family by appeal to the roles within the family. To the extent this appeal worked, the subservient were expected to be loyal, appreciative, and passive. To the extent this appeal worked, the liberty of one person to judge another, adult to adult, would be eroded. It is the great dignity of Locke's idealism that he expected dominance to abate when patrimonialism ended. Instead, it shifted its ground.

All through the 19th Century there were attempts to found communities on paternalistic principles. In the earlier part of the century, these attempts focused more on workhouses, asylums, and prisons than they did directly on factories. These institutions attempted to "reform" the characters of the inmates, rather than be simply places of punishment, as was true in the old regime. The "reforming" of character was thought necessary because the original formation in the family had failed; it was for this reason that in the 19th Century, asylums, workhouses, and prisons claimed for themselves the formal rights of *in loco parentis.* The concept of *in loco parentis* embodied in these reforming institutions is based on the following three assumptions. There are certain moral diseases which the normal family is too weak to cope with: insanity, sexual perversion, and the like. There are other diseases which the normal family, especially the normal poor family, causes: indolence, "despairing alcoholism," prostitution. If the surrogate parent is to succeed where the natural parent failed, the liberty of the person being treated must be radically curtailed. In the famous panopticon of Jeremy Bentham, for instance, the building is a set of cages placed in a circle around a central observation tower, so that the inmates can be constantly observed by the doctors, workhouse managers, or prison guards. The inmates cannot talk to each other, nor can they see if the guards are observing them at any one time, since Bentham designed an ingenious set of louvers and blinds for the central guard tower. (The plan of the panopticon, published in 1843, was used in the building of such institutions as the Rennes Prison in 1877 and the American federal penitentiary of Statesville in the early 20th Century.) There is control, but neither visual nor verbal interchange—or, rather, the initiation of all exchanges lies with the invisible guards, managers, and doctors. In this idea of an environment of moral reform, the surrogate parent acquires far more power than the natural parent, and the very idea of power is transformed into a one-sided control in which the subject is influenced but cannot in turn influence those who are taking care of him or her.

The original attempts to place industrial bosses *in loco parentis* to their employees intended nothing so harsh or, indeed, morally reforming. In the United States in the 1820's, there was great resistance to the building of large factories; the Jeffersonian idea remained strong that the evils of poverty in Europe would be imported to America if America's agricultural economy were supplanted by industrialism. In order to convince others that industrialism was not *per se* a source of corruption, the planners of mills in Waltham and Lowell, Massachusetts, decided to build industrial communities in which the wholesomeness of family values would be retained. The workers in these experiments were young women recruited into the mills for a few years only; they were expected to save up some money for the time when they married, and to leave the mills when they found a suitable husband. Unlike Robert Owen in his experimental factory at New Lanark in Scotland, the American entrepreneurs had no thought of morally improving the lives of the workers above the level of the families from which the working girls came; their purpose was simply to continue what most Americans thought was the essential integrity of the American farm family, and so rob industrialism of its sting.

To this end, the planners of Waltham arranged for reading groups, lectures, and Bible classes for the workers in the evenings. They provided the first comprehensive health care in this country for their employees. Most of all, in their capacities *in loco parentis,* the owners of the factories undertook to protect the morality of the young girls by building dormitories in which the workers would live, dormitories supervised by matrons who were on duty from the time the girls returned from the mills all through the night until the girls left again in the morning to work. In the design and operation of the dormitories, however, the power relationships of Bentham's panopticon reappear in fact, if not by intention. The dormitories were long, high-ceilinged rooms where the beds were arranged as in a hospital ward. The matrons were on duty in these rooms even while the girls slept; not only did they protect the girls from intruders, they kept the girls from escaping. Any sort of sexual or courting privacy was impossible. Moreover, the young men who came to visit the girls had to make appointments, and the matrons enforced rules regulating how long the appointments could be, and the conditions of meeting. The placement of parenting in a bureaucratic setting had the effect of increasing the power of the surrogate parent beyond that which normally prevailed in a home.

In France, the doctrine of *in loco parentis* had existed in education for hundreds of years before the 19th Century. (The principle existed in British education as well, but was never as strongly or elaborately articulated as in the French *collèges,* schools roughly equivalent to the British grammar school in the old regime.) During the first decades of the 19th Century, the doctrine of *in loco parentis* was applied to industrial life by the Abbé Lamennais and by Saint-Simon. The workshops Saint-Simon envisioned, which were briefly brought to life during the Revolution of 1848, were cooperative. Everyone in the workshop had a voice in decision-making. At the same time, there were leaders whom Saint-Simon calls the *pères du travail,* and these fathers, exactly like the father in a family dealing with his children, were to help the less able or more inexperienced workers decide what would be in their best interests. The workshop itself was to be a "foyer," a hearth or place for family life, which would be the center of the worker's entire existence; his or her biological family Saint-Simon envisaged eventually to be an appendage to the workshop. The *père du travail* would become, in Saint-Simon's words, by extension the counselor of the private family. Again a displacement, again a magnifying of the power of the surrogate parent.

The panopticon, New Lanark, the Waltham Mills, the Saint-Simonian workshops were all conceived against the grain of the individualistic economic ethos of the 19th Century. All these paternal experiments attempted to create a community. In the case of the industrial experiments, these versions of *in loco parentis* attempted to protect the conditions of work from the dominating influence of the market rate for wages, an influence which would determine, if left to itself, who would belong to the workshop, how decisions would be made, and the like. The criticism which hardheaded people, therefore, made of these early versions of paternalism was that they were costly, idealistic frills.

But by the end of the last century, these early ideas had been absorbed into the economy in such a way that they became profitable. Large company towns were built throughout the American East; outside of London, new factories were planned around Bristol, Birmingham, and Leeds so that the owners built housing for workers as well as the plants themselves; in the suburban development around Paris and Lyon, industrialists branched out into real estate development and the ownership of retail stores at which their employees shopped. Such innovations were quite hardheaded; large factories contain a big enough resident population that it becomes economically worthwhile for a producer to diversify into real estate or retail commerce.

These employers acquired more and more control over the lives of their employees. And they were, correspondingly, those most pressed to define principles for this control other than the free market; their employees lived, worked, and shopped in an environment which did not conform to anything resembling a free market. It was these employers who so frequently had recourse to the older notions of paternalism. They claimed that they were acting for their employees in the employees' own best interest; but, in contrast to the older Benthamite or Owenite schools, they claimed that mutual economic advantage to the employer and employee resulted, as well as a moral environment. Like the Walthamite industrialists, they worried about community services for their employees, but unlike the Walthamites, they argued openly that these services were morally valuable because happy workers were more productive and less strike-prone than unhappy ones.

It has sometimes been said that the corporate paternalism

of the steel towns of the American Midwest, or of the industrial suburbs of Leeds or Lyon, prefigures the state capitalism of the 20th Century. State capitalism is also a system in which work, welfare, and control of the lives of people in a community by a corporation are rolled into one. This view is not quite correct. Corporate paternalism was an attempt to grapple with two fundamental facts of the era of high capitalism. Family and work were no longer materially joined, as they were in the patrimonial era, or as they would be rejoined economically in the welfare state. The economic pressures which fragmented these realms also isolated individuals and abandoned them to the chance of the market, and again, the welfare state hopes to tame the excesses of the market. The corporate paternalists tried to weld family and work together symbolically through images of themselves as authorities. In doing so, they wanted communal cohesion, and from this stable community of workers to obtain higher rates of productivity.

They succeeded and failed. They created a bond of rejection with their employees, like the bonds discussed in Chapter One. One of the most dramatic examples of this bonding on a collective scale is the story of Pullman, Illinois, a town built by George Pullman around his massive sleeping-car factory in the late 19th Century.

## GEORGE PULLMAN

On May 12, 1894, the workers of the Pullman Palace Car Company went out on strike. The strike lasted three months, and before it had run its course had spread from the suburb on the south side of Chicago where the Pullman works were located to the whole nation. It was the first American experience of an attempted general strike, one of the first American experiences of the massive use of federal troops to put down civil disorder.

The most surprising thing about the strike was its origin. Pullman, Illinois, was thought to be one of the most successful of the company towns then being built in America, and Pullman was thought of as a leading employer. He combined something of the idealism of the Saint-Simonians with an almost machinelike capacity to coordinate a large-scale organization. The town of Pullman reflected these characteristics. Its architecture was a mixture of all the styles that Pullman thought most "nobly expressed their purposes"; a white clapboard New England church was therefore built next to, and at the same time as, a Gothic town hall. The factory works were Romanesque, and most of the workers' housing appears to have been late Georgian. On the other hand, the making of these architectural flights of fancy was done with the greatest efficiency; by the time of the strike, Pullman had built housing for 12,600 people. (Nationally, the Pullman Palace Car Company had 14,000 employees, of whom 5,500 worked in the town.) The terms of their existence were rigidly controlled, far more so than in other company towns of the era: a ban on alcohol was enforced through the stores and the town inn, both of which Pullman's company owned. There were also rules on cigarette smoking, and a curfew. Large, efficient, moralistic, iron-ruled—thus the town reflected the man.

Pullman's paternalism was most graphically shown in his views on the property of Pullman itself. No worker was allowed to buy a house, as this would have weakened Pullman's own control. In 1890, he made the following remarks to a visitor:

It is truly my intention to form another town, near this one, where each resident will build a cottage after his own inclination, suited to his own needs, and which will be his own. . . . I do not think the time has come yet for beginning this enterprise. If I had sold the sites to my workingmen at the beginning of the experiment, I should have run the risk of seeing families settle who are not sufficiently accustomed to the habits I wish to develop in the inhabitants of Pullman city, and all the good of my work would have been compromised by their presence. But today, after ten-years apprenticeship, several families recognize the advantages of them and will see that they are observed, wherever they may settle. Such families form the pick, and I hope to sell the building lands near the workshops to some of them, little by little.

The statement "I should have run the risk of seeing families settle who are not sufficiently accustomed to the habits I wish to develop in the inhabitants" is perhaps as succinct an expression of his attitude as one may find.

This attitude was one which the workers of Pullman initially understood and approved. For these workers were mostly immigrants from abroad; the town contained especially large numbers of Swedish and northern German peasants. Pullman transposed into the industrial world something of the patrimonial assumptions they had known in the old countries, patrimonial assumptions which were breaking up at home. (The destruction of the land base for a patrimonial system had by the middle of the 19th Century spread to the northernmost reaches of Europe.) Pullman did seem a protector, materially and emotionally. The fact that he treated his workers like children seemed only natural, given the way he used his power.

If for immigrants such a town was an oasis of order in the American desert, its protective features also appealed to native-born Americans who were having a hard time in the new industrial order. Here is the statement of a farm boy who moved first to Chicago and then to Pullman:

We had a little cottage on the west side [of Chicago] but there was mud on all sides of us, two beer saloons within a block, clouds of soft coal, poor sewerage, villainous water, and everything else that was bad and disagreeable. After our little girls were born I began to feel uncomfortable . . . there were many deaths in our section of the city from diphtheria and scarlet fever, and we found it next to impossible to keep everything clean. . . . I found I could work here [in Pullman] at wages fully equal to those paid in the city, and that I could rent a whole brick house with water and drainage . . . for $15 a month. . . . We have a clean and comfortable house and plenty of pure air. My children are healthy and, as far as my wife, she has seemed like a different woman.

Given an industrial community that afforded people such a feeling of protection, and was profitable to boot, why did one of the most dramatic strikes in the history of American capitalism occur here? At first glance, there appear two reasons.

Pullman was first of all an unstable community. The journalist Richard Ely observed:

> Nobody regards Pullman as a real home, and, in fact, it can scarcely be said that there are more than temporary residents of Pullman. One woman told the writer that she had been in Pullman two years, and that there were only three families among her acquaintances who were there when she came. Her reply to the question "It is like living in a great hotel, is it not?" was "We call it camping out."

The more industrious workers at Pullman's works bought houses for themselves outside the community as soon as they could; the "good children" escaped his control, since they wanted to own, and he refused to give up his paternal power by selling. Those who remained in Pullman were people who, for one reason or another, could not accumulate the capital for homeownership. They felt like second-class citizens, resenting both the successful workers and the company which refused to convert their rent payments into an equity investment. Pullman never anticipated that his foreign workers would regard the ownership of private property as so important. They did so not only because ownership provided material security, but also because it was a symbol of assimilation in the new culture, of throwing down roots. This was the irony of George Pullman's paternalism: he could retain his power over the physical look of the community, over who belonged to it, and over how they lived only as long as he denied his charges the opportunity to own. Private property threatened the paternalistic controls of this very successful capitalist.

The second source of rebellion applied to all the workers in Pullman's plant. Paternalism personalizes the human relations in work: I, your employer, care about you and will take care of you. This, however, is a dangerous formula. When things go wrong, it isn't the abstractions like market stress which the employees hold responsible. It is the employer. They hold him as personally responsible for his power. The leader of the Pullman strikers, Thomas Heathcoate, remarked after the strike: "The employees were very well disposed toward Mr. Pullman until the action of the last management [by which Heathcoate meant foremen several removes from Pullman in the company structure] seemed to estrange the men from Mr. Pullman." Not only were the faults of his subordinates ultimately his fault, fluctuations in the economy outside the company to which management adjusted, like changes in demand which require temporary layoffs, became interpreted as Mr. Pullman's personal betrayal of his charges. This is perfectly logical as a perception. He asserted personal control over them; therefore, he became personally responsible for what happened to them. The result is to transform the experience of economic stress into a highly emotional matter. One Pullman worker, for instance, remarked of his immediate boss, "The treatment we have received from the foreman of the company has been worse than the slaves ever received in the South." To an outsider, this is a patent absurdity; to an insider, it is again logical because work had been made so personal.

Paternalism contradicted the individualism of the time, expressed in the desire to own private property. It exerted an immensely personal control over the lives of the workers; when conflicts arose, the backfire was also immensely personal. But this process entrenched itself in society in a manner we began to explore in the last chapter. The way the paternalistic metaphor is constructed invites negation. The acts of negating knit the workers and bosses together, however. It became difficult for the workers to form cooperative associations with one another, to act fraternally and effectively. All their energies were concentrated on that highly charged emotional relationship with the boss.

As early as 1885, American observers of Pullman had been trying to understand this knot. In that year Richard Ely wrote a celebrated article for *Harper's Magazine* in which the town is portrayed as the model for the totally controlled society which George Orwell would later depict in *1984*. Pullman's fatherly attitude, however well meant, was the source, in Ely's view, of the loss of freedom workers experienced in the town. A more probing analysis of the connection between fathering and adult power over adults appeared some years after the Pullman strike, in an article the social worker Jane Addams published in *Survey Magazine* on November 2, 1912. It is a remarkable study of the assertion and negation of personal authority in modern society.

In "A Modern Lear," Addams probes the idea that Pullman was a paternalistic employer by comparing Shakespeare's King Lear to the modern industrialist. What unites the two is that their benevolence invited rejection, Lear at the hands of his daughters, Pullman at the hands of his workers. Her method was metaphorical—Pullman is a Lear—because her subject was "A boss is a father." But Addams was also seeking to understand why in the industrial world the rebellious children do not take the place of their surrogate parents, but become ever more dependent upon them.

She compares Lear and Pullman in four ways. First, in a paternal relationship, one person is authorized to control the boundaries of reality for other people. To put the matter in her elegant prose:

> Lear had doubtless swung a bauble before Cordelia's baby eyes that he might have the pleasure of seeing the little pink and tender hands stretched for it ... it was impossible for him to calmly watch his child developing beyond the strength of his own mind and sympathy

When Cordelia does rebel against his control of her life, Addams says:

> It was new to him that his child should be moved by a principle outside of himself, which even his imagination could not follow; that she had caught the notion of an existence so vast that her relationship as a daughter was but part of it.

It is this same sense of being authorized to control the boundaries of the reality of others which led Pullman to dictate when his workers could be on the streets, why they could not take a drink, even how they should dress.

As long as the workers, like the little girl, accept this control as only right and proper, then the bond is not subject to much conscious scrutiny. But the moment the girl or the workers can see beyond the limits of reality laid down by the King or the boss, then the very fact that the father has had control of the gates of reality comes to the forefront of consciousness. It takes this glimpse beyond the gates to make people confront just how deep is his control. The girl or the workers confront it in rebellious rage; the King, the industrialist realize how deeply they have tried to implant their own values in other people's lives when they feel betrayed. "I was like a father to them," Pullman lamented, puzzled and hurt that despite this they could go on strike.

Jane Addams comes here upon the simplest and subtlest element of the connection. Paternalism draws on the reality-control fathers have over their children. In any family, that control is neither pure love nor pure power; altruism and egoism are joined. In Hawthorne's words, "Benevolence is here the twin of pride." This join becomes conscious when the children become enraged by being so controlled and the parent feels betrayed by their rebellion. At this moment of crisis, because all parties in it have become aware of its constitution, it is fully felt.

Both Lear and Pullman expected their charges to show appreciation by being obedient and deferential. Now it might easily be objected that here surely the link between an industrialist and an ordinary father, not a Lear, breaks down, for ordinary fathers do not make such one-sided demands upon their children. In her essay, Jane Addams makes a most interesting response to this problem. Lear, as she points out, is aware that in giving away his kingdom before he has to, he is acting "beyond his measure" as a father. Similarly, Pullman had heaped extraordinary benefits upon those toward whom he had no duty recognized by common consent . . . had not only exceeded the righteousness of the employer, but . . . had worked out original and striking methods for lavishing goodness and generosity. . . .

Indeed, she observes,

. . . the president had been almost persecuted for this goodness by the more utilitarian members of his company and had at one time imperiled his business reputation for the sake of the benefactions to his town. . . .

Both men had gone "beyond the measure" of duty or law. Interestingly, because Pullman did more than necessary as an employer, people described him as a paternal boss. Two images: Lear as an exceptional father; Pullman who needed to be an exceptional boss in order to be seen at all as a father.

These two images are clues about the metaphor involved in paternalism. In associating "father" and "boss," paternalism magnifies the scale and power of the "father" term. It is a Lear who explains to us Pullman as a father. Similarly, in the asylums or reformatories of the earlier part of the century, in Bentham's panopticon, in the factories of Lowell and Waltham, the element of parental control was inflated beyond its "natural measure." This process is very different from the mirroring of family roles in social life psychoanalysts are prone to believe in. *In loco parentis* or the belief in the fatherliness of a boss does something to our very concept of father. In particular, the element of egoistic benevolence in fathering is magnified. In Bentham's panopticon, those in the central tower are given extraordinary powers over their charges in order to reform them, to do them some good, but this benevolent power is entirely egoistic; the charges cannot speak to their masters, they cannot even see them. Isolated, uninterrupted, unchallenged, the masters do good. In Pullman's town, the workers are not allowed to own property, so that they do not challenge their employer or interrupt him in the doing of his good works. This is egoistic benevolence, magnified beyond what is usual in family life.

Comparison of behavior between roles of different scale, between a father with one or two children and a boss with several thousand charges, works when elements in the small scene are selected, then used in the comparison. Magnification rather than reduction is the principle of their use. The consequence is that a direct human encounter—child and parent—becomes the material for an image of authority which is dominating, intimidating. It becomes a magnified reality, but based on experience with which the subordinate can identify. In the course of being magnified, the role is transformed; only certain elements are blown up, so that the role becomes a distorted version of the original small scale. This is why Addams's comparison of Pullman to Lear is more apt than if she had compared him to a man who would expect from his children some sort of balance between deference and independence.

This is also why the work of imagination in a paternalistic culture is so different from that of other forms of male domination. In a society where all social relations are consciously perceived as family, people can equate fathers, uncles, grandfathers directly with different kinds of rulers. There is no need for a principle of transformation. "The ruler is your father" or "The ruler is your grandfather" is a literal rather than metaphorical statement. In societies where lineage does not chart human relationships, some rule of transformation must be used when associations between family and politics, work, or warfare are made. The magnification of the small-scale role is a common way to do this because it starts with what is concrete and immediate in each person's experience and literally builds it up to the point where it will be serviceable in giving a meaning to persons who are distant and remote. Those persons become immediate—you know what they are like—and awesome—they are super-fathers.

Because paternalism is more complicated than a simple comparison of kings, union leaders, or bosses to fathers, the feelings aroused by a paternal figure are correspondingly more complicated than the feelings aroused by a father. Shame is a good example of this.

A child does not need to be ashamed of itself when it obeys its father. But when outsiders like Richard Ely criticized the social life of the town of Pullman, they frequently alluded to the fact that it was shameful that one adult would treat another as if he were a father. This is quite different from the assumptions made in a patriarchal or patrimonial society. One adult obeying another in these societies is usually no more shameful than a child obeying its parent. Within the family, on the other side, a father challenged by his children need not necessarily feel humiliated if the children succeed in resisting him; he may in fact be pleased they have the guts to stand up to him. When fathering is magnified into the peculiar image of paternalism, resistance makes the benevolent ego feel exposed; Pullman worried that he could not hold his head up in the business community after the workers went on strike.

Egoistic benevolence magnified, passive deference demanded, shame introduced into obedience: this catalogue of evils may make it appear that paternalism is wholly a matter of malign intent. We would miss the pathos of authority in the era of high capitalism if we were to think so. Pullman went to great effort to offer his workers something more than a job. Throughout the 19th Century, paternalistic controls were similarly motivated by a desire to make personal, face-to-face contacts—to make a community—in an economic system always pulling people into paths of individual striving and mutual competition. Moreover, the recourse to the family, rather than to the Church, or to the military, had a purpose: allusions to the family are attempts to make these personal contacts warm, rather than a matter of piety or shared aggressiveness. The metaphor aims at intimacy. The pathos of this search for an image of personal authority is that the intent is perverted by the conditions of economic power which give the image its shape. Pullman's workers come to respond to the form of his offer, rather than to his motive. They can do no other; they must negate the terms of his benevolence if they do not want to sink into abject dependence.

When I was a student, I came across a remark in Ruggiero's great *History of European Liberalism* which seemed to me incomprehensible. He observed that the tragedy of 19th Century industrialism was not that the powerful were oppressive, or that the subordinate were insufficiently armed for defense; this is always the case, it is what domination means. To Ruggiero, the tragedy of modern industrialism was that the subordinate could never transcend the terms of power used by their oppressors. No day of judgement, no apocalypse, would finally settle scores; the weak could resist only by being the negative of whatever the powerful wanted them to be. The conclusion of Jane Addams's essay makes graphically clear what Ruggiero meant, and why, therefore, the strong and the weak become locked into each other's lives.

We remember the vivid scene in Shakespeare's play when King Lear demands of Cordelia some token of her deference, appreciation, and love. He does not demand much, in fact; just a few words. But Cordelia responds to his plea with nothing. In Addams's words:

> It seems to us a narrow conception that would break thus abruptly with the past, and would assume that her father had no part in her new life. We want to remind her that "pity, memory, and faithfulness are natural ties."

This observation, if true, then raises some disturbing questions about Cordelia's parallel, Pullman's workers.

Most sensible people today can identify with workers striking to better their economic position; most people can at least sympathetically understand the impulse to challenge paternal authority which may occur in the process. Addams's point is that something valuable will be lost at this breaking point. The workers are then against the boss, for themselves. The possessive appetites are aroused. Addams's words are eloquent:

That a newly acquired sense of possession should result in the barbaric, the incredible scenes of bitterness and murder, which were King Lear's portion, is not without a reminder of the barbaric scenes in our political and industrial relationships, when the sense of possession, to obtain and to hold, is aroused on both sides.

The negation of authority does not transcend the ethos of capitalism: "possession" is the ruling term. The vision of a better social order, or a more truly responsive and nurturing authority, of *better* authority, is not germinated by this resistance.

The work of Charles Tilly and Edward Shorter on French labor protest in the 19th Century has shown that workers in company towns were slower to organize themselves than those who lived in towns with many industries, or industries not controlled by paternalistic bosses. A study by Daniel Walkowitz, *Worker City, Company Town,* shows that workers experienced a similar difficulty in 19th Century industrial America. The potency of paternalism is more, however, than a matter of deflecting protest. One consequence of this highly charged conflict is that the worker can reject anyone who reaches out to him in the name of helping him. A graphic instance appears in the following recollection from a worker who lived in Pullman in the 1880's:

> After the strike was over I went back to the Sleeping Palace works. They still came around, you know, the socialists, trying to start things up again. The Debs men. [Eugene Debs, the leading American socialist, was involved in organizing workers during the Pullman strike.] They told us Pullman was a fox, he'd tricked us. But I was through with the whole thing. I believed Pullman once, why should I believe in Debs?

The socialists are no more able to dramatize Pullman as a fox than Pullman was able to legitimate himself as a father. Learning to disbelieve, *per se,* is what the worker took away from the original experience. Pullman and Debs became equally subjected to that process: "I believed Pullman once, why should I believe in Debs?" Because what Debs says is true? No, the truth is in the negating. This is personal confrontation reduced to its lowest common denominator: a struggle for self-possession. The content of authority, what authority should be, is cast aside.

Paternalism is something more than a passing phase in the history of capitalism. The fate of this image of authority in the modern world is, in part, ironic. It has passed into the language of revolutionary socialism. From the 1920's on, Soviet Russian leaders began to make use of it, and the usage has been repeated in more recent socialist regimes.

The blood tie is a classical emblem of patriarchal kingship. In official Russian poems commissioned in the early 1930's, it reappeared as a metaphor of revolutionary solidarity. A typical poster slogan was "All have in their blood a drop of Lenin's blood." In Elena Katerli's novel *The Stozharovs,* published in 1948, the blood image reappeared again, now as a metaphor for the hierarchy which binds the people to Stalin:

> It seems to me . . . that in each Communist there is a kind of particle of Stalin. In any true Communist, of course. And this helps him to be sure and calm, to know what to do, to what everything will lead if he acts as the Party commands. A Communist [is] a leader in everything and everywhere, a teacher of life for the people.

Whereas Lenin was often depicted in posters and official poems in conjunction with his spouse, Krupskaya, Stalin is depicted alone, often holding the sun high in one hand and the moon lower in the other—the moon being an ancient feminine symbol in Georgian folklore. Indeed, the folklore of magical kingship is transposed directly into the industrial world, as in this official poem of the 1940's:

> Where he [Stalin] stepped, a trace remained, each step a new town, a bridge, a railroad . . . town houses, like cliffs; over the whole earth he sowed things which are stronger than granite.

It might be said that these paternal images, touched with blood, are quite natural in societies like Stalin's Russia or Mao's China. Socialism sprang not from a decayed capitalist order but from at best an infant one; the masses of people were still bound to semi-feudal ways. But the more salient issue is the ideology of socialism itself. Everything in Engels and Marx's version of a socialist remaking of society aimed at eliminating the "magical presences," as Engels called them, of the authorities who rule *in loco parentis*. However, Joseph Stalin is ideologically George Pullman's true heir; in Stalin's own words, "The state is a family, and I am your father." The authority Bentham and others intended for capitalist bureaucracies was expropriated by the enemy of capitalism.

The reason this occurred has to do in part with the very nature of the revolutionary claim: a fundamental change has occurred in the structure of society. This claim is dangerous. What happens if something goes wrong afterward? In Stalin's Russia it was safe to notice bureaucratic inefficiency or failure; it was dangerous to notice something in the structure of the bureaucracy—that is, the structure of state power—which caused the failure to occur. To see a connection between structure and function risks challenging the following first principle (stated by A. Rumjancev, in the Moscow journal *Kommunist,* during the "thaw" of 1956):

> Members of ruling organs in the economy, as it is well known, are elected on a mandate from the working class. . . . The organs of the State are under the control of the vanguard of the workers— the Communist Party—as are the trade unions and other social organizations. The material process of work, by its very nature, seeks to subordinate the will of all to the will of one authorized by socialist society and responsible to it. This suits the interests of all workers. And sensible workers cannot but submit themselves to that which presents the general interest.

In order to avoid challenging this first principle, bureaucratic failure is laid at the door of individual bureaucrats. This is the key to the place of personality in all totalitarian regimes. Since it is dangerous to see connections between structure and function, personalities are brought to the fore to explain disasters: Hess's defection was thought by loyal Nazis to be the clue to the reason Germany began losing the war; the Gang of Four is the reason for the recent problems of Chinese socialism. Conversely, personal authority during secure periods is celebrated. When a leader's picture is in every office or schoolroom, you know who incarnates all the appeals for higher production, reorganization of the cement industry, and the like. This is power with a distinctly human face. When the pictures are removed from the offices, factories, and schools, you also know what went wrong; he did. He failed to live up to the revolutionary ideals, but the revolution remains intact.

In the era of high capitalism, the paternalist image was an attempt to bridge a gulf between economic individualism and the desire for community. It is not surprising, therefore, that revolutionary regimes which have expropriated this image can officially declare the conflict between individualism and community to be over. At the height of the Stalinist era, the journal *Sem'ya i Shkola* (Family and School) proclaimed in April 1948: "The socialist regime liquidated the tragedy of loneliness from which men of the capitalist world suffer." In 1977, the unfortunate Pol Pot, leader of Free Kampuchea, succinctly declared: "There is only community here." The leader is the solvent. He incarnates the community; every person, as in the blood imagery, partakes of his being.

In addition to this ironic transfer from high capitalism to bureaucratic socialism, paternalism persists in Western industrial societies as well, not only in businesses like IBM, but also in politics. In America and Great Britain we are coming to know paternalism in a most peculiar form: the leader who reaches over the heads of the bureaucracy, as it were, to establish personal relations with the people. The government over which he presides becomes the common enemy of president and people alike. The leader will care for the people personally as the formal machinery of the welfare state cannot. Moreover he will set a moral example, serve as a "role-model," in the jargon of the social sciences. While it may be appropriate for a parent to serve as a role-model, it is curious for a president or prime minister to do so as the avowed enemy of the state apparatus. Or perhaps it is quite clever. The leader rules, but is absolved from taking responsibility for the engines of rule, the government bureaucracy. Clever but dangerous. As in the socialist bureaucracies, if policies go wrong the leader is personally blamed. As a high government official in England once observed, it is "safer" to have a prime minister who is the enemy of the established bureaucracy than a ruler who speaks through it; the Establishment may be perceived by the people as no good, but when government fails it is hard to call the gray men to account.

What is the bond of paternalism, then; what sort of personal connections does it make? It is a bond of metaphor—and I mean by that word to indicate how paternalism is perceived and how it is mutually felt.

## THE BONDS OF A METAPHOR

"Pullman is a King Lear," "A boss is a father," "The Catholic Church is a mother," "The nation is a home," *das Vaterland, la patrie*—all are, semantically, metaphors. In the last two, the joining of father and country has proceeded to its ultimate state, a single noun.

What is a metaphor? Classical writers believed it was the joining of two words or phrases not usually connected and that the purpose of this joining was purely aesthetic. Aristotle thought metaphors were a way of producing "delight" in the use of language, and Cicero believed metaphors infused their principal subject with "blood." These classical writers established a tradition of viewing metaphor as a decoration, in Max Black's phrase, rather than an instrument of thought.

Clearly, this classical mode of thought is not all there is to be said. "A ruler is a father" or *das Vaterland* involves such basic intellectual processes as discovering a similarity or making an analogy. But the classical bias persists in much writing on metaphors and in everyday thought. When we say "What you mean when you say *das Vaterland* is that a nation is like a father in this way and that way and yet again another way," we assume that the metaphor can be directly translated into non-metaphorical terms. Such a mode of thinking denies the intrinsic meaning of metaphors, since they can be so literally translated into non-metaphors. The metaphor still appears only as an adornment of another meaning.

I suppose poets would never have taken much to these views about metaphor. In the last half-century, philosophers of science and students of the social uses of language have become increasingly sceptical about them as well. They have come to believe that in making a mental model of a physical process or a social phenomenon, there comes a point when thinking metaphorically is the only way to think at all. This view may be traced to a famous statement by I. A. Richards: "When we use a metaphor we have two thoughts of different things active together and supported by a single word, or phrase, whose meaning is a resultant of their interaction." Put another way, a metaphor creates a meaning greater than the sum of its parts, because the parts interact. The terms of a metaphor have meaning in relation to each other which they do not have apart. This is how metaphors may establish social relationships: the parts of the metaphor may be different social classes, or different roles in society. The whole creates the special meaning for the parts.

Paternalism is such a metaphor. Father and leader, when joined, change the meaning each has alone. In the text of Jane Addams we have seen the substance of this mutual change: Pullman-Lear works by isolating an element in the father's role, his egoistic benevolence, then magnifying its importance beyond what Shakespeare called "the natural measure" of the family and what social-science jargon calls the normative scale of the role. Once this is done, so that the concept of father is an active ingredient in the metaphor, then the concept of boss is also transformed. It is infused with a sense of emotional potency, of the power to dominate the affections of others, which the term "boss" alone could never have. In the terminology of Max Black, the magnification of father provides the "frame" for the metaphor within which "boss" becomes the "focal word."

This linguistic action of metaphor has consequences in how people feel and behave toward one another. Most important of these consequences is that the fear of a person in power may be magnified. Formal control over a thousand people is joined to experiences of face-to-face control each person has felt deeply in the family. It is awesome to think of a person affecting many people in an intimate way. It is the work of metaphor which makes that awesome juncture.

In the same way, metaphor gives contradictions in a society a sense of coherence. In the 19th Century, "father" stands for a world of solid moral values and probity, "boss" stands for heartless amoral striving. The action of metaphor, Paul Ricoeur has observed in a recent work, *La Métaphore Vive,* is not to prefer one side over the other, not to take sides. Rather, a metaphor confronts dissonant meanings with one another, so that each is changed by the other. This is why societies experiencing tensions so often express their beliefs in ways which to an outsider seem absurd; the outsider, considering the meaning of the expression "Think of me as your father," sees the dissonance of the parts but ignores the semantic process that makes them a whole.

It would be wrong to consider metaphorical thinking as inherently oppressive. Metaphors are put to oppressive uses. When they are, their structure permits certain things to be done—to magnify the potency of an authority figure, for example, or join dissonant experiences. But only certain kinds of metaphor can be used this way. If an industrialist were to say "Think of me as your little girl," we would probably send him off to a clinic; the metaphor makes no calls on our credence. Metaphors for domination are restricted in two ways.

First, in such a metaphor both of the terms must refer to a comparable form of domination. Father refers to a form of control, as does boss; little girl does not. The metaphor can work the other way around; the weak may be called sheep. Either way, a society must have rules for conceiving of power in stratified levels, and both the frame and the focal word of the metaphor must be on the same level. The two terms, no matter how dissonant, then have a reason to be associated.

The second restriction is more ominous. Any imaginative act which joins dissonant parts would seem, on the face of it, to make consciousness more complex. However, metaphor can be used so that it simplifies reality. An instance from the case study explored in the last chapter: Miss Bowen reported that once, after she and her second black lover had a long discussion of all the elements in their relationship, the man said to her, "Basically, I'm your toy." Putting "I" and "toy" together here is a way of radically simplifying what the "I" means in the relation.

Metaphors of domination simplify in exactly this way. Considered in itself, family life is much more complex than the egoistic, benevolent power of a father. Work, too, is much more complex than the personal feelings between a boss and his or her employees. The metaphor, by joining both, narrows the sense of each. A prime example: Hitler once called the Jews insects. The metaphor simplifies the term "Jew" so that it stands for something small, crawling, repulsive; "insect" also acquires a restricted meaning. We do not think of bees or butterflies in this pairing; we think of maggots or spiders. A common level between frame and focal word; a simplification of the meaning of each term: these restrictions make it possible for metaphors to brutalize the intelligent understanding people have of the conditions of power which rule their lives. Plato feared with good reason the importing of poetic rhetoric into politics.

One reads ruefully passages like the following from John Stuart Mill's *Principles of Political Economy,* published during the revolutions of 1848: "Of the working men, at least in the more advanced countries of Europe, it may be pronounced as certain that the patriarchal . . . system of government is one to which they will not again be subject. . . . Whatever advice, exhortation, or guidance must henceforth be tendered to them as equals." The first part of Mill's statement describes an important event in the history of authority in the 19th Century; the second is a non sequitur.

The work of metaphor was to provide one different outcome. There has been an attempt to join in an image two domains which are in the modern world materially and circumstantially quite different from each other: family and work. The way they are joined together transforms the meaning of each. The personal image of authority which results is both potent and fragile. The act of destroying this metaphor leads to the conviction that freedom lies in the very act of disbelieving.

I spoke in the last chapter of the bonds of resentment which could attach the rebellious or discontent to authorities. Not only cowardice, the fear of punishment, or terror can make these bonds, but something which cuts deeper beneath the surface of human relations. To confront someone is to know him or her, and know one's own place in the world. What one fears about others may be their potency, a strength one cannot imagine doing without. In the construction of the paternalistic metaphor, many of the elements involved in making this bond appear in one way or another. The potency of the superior is magnified. Something solid is made of the dissonances of society; they are welded together in a unit and have in metaphor a sense that the parts cannot have alone. But beyond all this paternalism touches on those fantasies of disappearance explored in the preceding chapter. Those fantasies are delaying mechanisms: if only you were gone, it would be all right, but delay your moment of going because I will be bereft. We know that those who lived under the yoke of paternalistic authorities were slow to rise against them, slower in the 19th Century than workers who rose against their masters in more cosmopolitan milieux. But the element which matters here most is the sense of being bereft if finally the rising comes. The comment of the Pullman worker "I believed in Pullman, why should I believe in Debs?" is the statement of a depressed man. Negation is truth—but what stands accused is not an act of misplaced faith but faith at all.

The strength of this metaphor lies ultimately in the substance of what it fuses. It is a fusion of care and power; more accurately, if more embarrassingly, love and power. One definition of an authority is precisely someone who will use his strength to care for others. When we observe, therefore, the difficulty with which the subjects of power push away those who claim to care for them, or the depression which follows the act of rejection, we are observing people who have lost a sense of some humane value of power.

Of course those who rejected paternalism were right to do so: paternalistic authorities hold out a false love to their subjects. False because the leader cares for these subjects only insofar as it serves his interests. Unlike a patrimonial figure, he makes a gift of his resources to others. The terms of this gift are wholly in his control. Pullman was willing to make the gift only on the condition that his charges be gratefully passive. When Stalin declared "I am your father," he spoke a language which has no resemblance to exchanges between a real father and his children; there is no tolerance of their crankiness, no willingness to sacrifice himself—above all, no encouragement of their independence. Or if we take a less extreme example, there is the famous advice to a new manager from the former head of a paternalistic American magazine empire: "Spoil them! Like spoiled children they'll grouse about you all the time and jump the moment you call." Jane Addams had to choose a Lear for an image that would fit Pullman as a father. It might be said of all these cases that the surrogates were bad fathers rather than false ones, but I think this is too tepid. There is a promise of nurturance made in paternalistic ideologies, and the essential quality of nurturance is denied: that one's care will make another person grow stronger.

The belief that power ought to have something to do with nurturance is one which religion traditionally championed in adult social life. The Renaissance monk Savonarola spoke of the necessity of giving power a conscience. I suppose one might say that the joining of power and care is "only" idealistic now because this critical conscience is moribund. But we are also coming to see in modern society just what power without nurturance looks like. Power has been as well transformed into another image of authority, at the opposite pole from paternalism. Instead of false concern, this new authority expressed no care for others at all. This is the authority of an autonomous figure, and the subject of the next chapter.

# 3

# Autonomy, an Authority Without Love

Paternalism stands at one extreme of the images of authority in modern society. It is power exercised for the good of others. No hereditary obligation binds a person to do so, nor do religious injunctions. The care for others is the authority's gift, and he will bestow it only so long as it serves his interests. At the other extreme are images of authority which make no pretense of care. These images are more subtle, because they do not seem at first glance to concern the control one person exercises over another. They are images of an autonomous person.

In the physical sciences, autonomy means self-sufficing. In social life no one can be. A much older, Renaissance definition of autonomy is of a person who is self-possessed. This definition comes closer to describing the spell of autonomy. Personal mastery is rare; it commands respect. But a self-possessed person does more than elicit respect. The one who appears master of himself has a strength which intimidates others.

Paternalism arose in the last century as a way of creating a community out of new materials of power: work severed from the household, an open labor market, expanding cities. Autonomy is the heir of the contrary direction of individualism which these new materials of power might take. But the heir has enriched his legacy. The essence of 19th Century individualism lay in being left alone: if you were poor, as an individual you were abandoned to your fate; if you were rich, no one had the right to stop you from becoming more so. In a world where material differences are becoming less glaring, in which services and skills are the coins of exchange, autonomy is more stable. One person is needed by others more than he or she needs them. They need something which he or she has learned to be rather than something the person owns. A 19th Century plutocrat could lose on the stock market one day, and the next be subject to the scorn of people who had a few hours before deferred to him. But a doctor or a skilled bureaucrat has trained and developed himself; his very nature is what he possesses, and what other people need.

Autonomy takes a simple and a complex form. The simple form is the possession of skills. Modern society is sometimes labeled as a "skill society" because of the premium on technical expertise. Indeed, Daniel Bell has argued that technical expertise and innovation have become the modern forms of capital; expertise is like the cash of the 19th Century entrepreneur in that whoever has it can be independent. Autonomy also takes a more complicated form, one which anyone who has worked in the upper levels of a bureaucracy will recognize. This is a matter of character structure rather than skill. For instance, a manager is promotable not when he does just one specific task well but when he can coordinate the work of a number of people, each with his or her own expert skills. Bureaucracies have invented a whole host of images to describe the qualities of such a manager. Of course, he has to get along with other people. To direct his subordinates rather than be imprisoned by all the particular demands they make on him, however, he has to possess a set of attitudes which keep him independent, self-possessed, more influencing than reactive. This bundle of personality traits divorced of any particular technical expertise creates the complex form of autonomy. It is sought not only in managers, but in evaluating the future prospects of children in school, and in evaluating lower-level workers. Autonomous character structure means a person has the ability to be a good judge of others because he or she is not desperate for their approval. Self-control thus appears as a strength, a strength of calmness and above-the-storm which makes telling others what to do seem natural.

When a person is needed by others more than he needs them, he can afford to be indifferent to them. If the bureaucrat ignores the distress of the welfare client filling out complicated forms, if the doctor treats his clients like bodies rather than persons, these very acts of indifference maintain dominance. In the complex form of autonomy, keeping cool when others make demands on you or challenge you is a way of keeping the upper hand. Of course, few people set out to be rude or callous. But autonomy removes the necessity of dealing with other people openly and mutually. There is an imbalance; they show their need for you more than you show your need for them. This puts you in control.

In reacting to this dominance, those in need can come to perceive autonomous figures as authorities. The fear and awe of experts is a familiar sentiment, most notably as it concerns doctors. The perception of something authoritative about an autonomous character structure is perhaps more perverse. Someone who is indifferent arouses our desire to be recognized; we want this person to feel we matter enough to be noticed. We may provoke or denounce him, but the point is to get him to respond. Afraid of his indifference, not understanding what it is which keeps him aloof, we come to be emotionally dependent. Every reader of Proust is given the most exact lesson in this process as it concerns erotic authority. Indifference elevates the loved one, Proust writes; the loved one's sheer distance makes of him or her an unattainable ideal. Thus the narrator becomes Albertine's "slave." If the entreaty is noticed, the regard returned, then the spell is broken. Proust thinks of breaking the autonomy of another to be like recovery from a "disease of submission."

Through surveys of professional prestige and of desirable personality traits, it is possible to define rather precisely who is now perceived to be autonomous. The most prestigious occupations in the United States, Great Britain, and Italy—countries where the phenomenon has been most intensively studied—are occupations like medicine, law, or research science. The respondents give these jobs high status because the people in them are perceived to be able to work only according to their own light and interests. Corporate managers are lower on the scale insofar as they are seen to be dependent on other people. Many highly skilled craft occupations, like carpentering, are accorded higher status than white-collar pursuits in which a person may wear a tie to work and have a secretary but is essentially a cog in a bureaucratic machine. A study of "desirable personality traits," carried out among American college students, lists two at the top: openness and self-reliance; then, in decreasing order, perseverance, belief in a goal, assertiveness. Trust and loyalty are near the bottom. A somewhat similar study in England shows openness and self-determination at the top, trust rather higher up, and willingness to share at the bottom.

The leading candidates on these lists of desirable personality traits are obviously in conflict. The conflict exists because this image of authority arouses a mixed response. Autonomous persons may be strong, but they can also be destructive. For instance, we have an adverse reaction constantly about autonomous figures in bureaucracies, but don't realize we are having it. We feel the indifference of people in positions of bureaucratic power in terms of something else: impersonality. Max Weber expressed this reaction in the following way:

Its specific nature . . . develops the more perfectly the more the bureaucracy is "dehumanized," the more completely it succeeds in eliminating from official business, love, hatred, and all purely personal, irrational, and emotional elements which escape calculation.

There is a missing person here: the subject reacting to this coldness. That subject is also part of the bureaucracy; he or she is reacting to blankness on the faces of those in control. Usually explanations of impersonality disregard the character and behavior of the powerful, and talk about another cause: size. Government is too big or hospitals are too large to be humane. This is itself a curiously impersonal explanation; if only the size of things were smaller, the quality of human relations would improve.

The whole history of 19th Century paternalism offers lesson after lesson in how to create an intimate, personal environment which is oppressive, and in which the powerful are indifferent to the desires of their charges. Pullman, personally known to his employees, was indifferent to their desires to buy their own homes. The nature of power relations, how they are perceived and organized, is what determines a complex phenomenon like indifference. A purely quantitative idea, suggesting that the size of institutions leads to their impersonality which in turn leads to the practice of indifference, is much too simplistic. When we use the word "impersonality" to explain experiences of being ignored, we are trying, poorly, to say what autonomy feels like to others.

In this chapter I want to look at four facets of autonomous authority. First is its relation to discipline, both the discipline the autonomous person imposes upon himself and that which he imposes upon other people. Second is the bond that can be built between an autonomous person and a subordinate who nonetheless reacts negatively to this discipline. Third is how the controls autonomous authorities exercise over others are coming to be more veiled and protected in modern bureaucratic ideologies. Finally I wish to look at the belief in autonomy as a form of freedom.

## DISCIPLINE

We have a good idea of what Stalin has in mind when he declares "I am your father." He is going to force other people to do his bidding; he asserts his right to do so because he is the collective father. After a while people will habitually obey; the habit of obedience is discipline. Matters are less clear in the case of the chairman of an English manufacturing firm who made the following speech to his manual laborers:

> Each of us has his place in the company. I do my job as well as I can, and I hope you each do yours to the best of your ability. If we all work hard, I think we can all work profitably and harmoniously together. I certainly don't want to interfere with your work. Frankly, I don't understand the intricacies of what most of you do, just as you don't understand the complexities of decision-making I have to face. We must respect our mutual distances.

The employer eschews his ability to force other people to do his bidding; indeed, he declares he wouldn't know what to tell them to do. The closest he comes to a threat is his sentence which begins, "If we all work hard . . ." But it is weak. He is preaching voluntary self-discipline for the sake of the firm: discipline without force.

However, there is a hidden, coercive message. It has to do with how likely he or they are to become self-disciplined. Hard work at something intricate is the product of education, training, and the development of character. The higher up the social scale one is, the more access to education and training one has. Therefore one is more likely to succeed in having skills to control. In terms of simple autonomy, the "capital" of skills is greater. What does it mean to control this resource?

In the era of high capitalism, self-discipline had a clear meaning. There is a famous portrait of Mrs. Jay Gould, wife of the American millionaire, wearing a half-million-dollar pearl choker. Mrs. Gould remarked to the photographer that she wore it only in front of strangers, and that she was "afraid" of her necklace. She certainly was not afraid to spend money. Up and down the ranks of the bourgeoisie, people were frantically buying, and displaying publicly what they had bought. People had to show what they possessed in order for other people to know where they stood in society; goods were social markers. But the fear was that if one enjoyed one's possessions, one would, as the Victorian phrase put it, be consumed by pleasure. The sexual allusion is apt: have it but don't enjoy it. Someone who enjoys an object is likely to be destroyed by pleasure, and to squander his or her resources. The disciplinary task of the individual was therefore to work hard to own, to take pride in possession, but not to succumb to material sensuality.

The discipline of an autonomous person today is rather different. Autonomy arises out of self-expression rather than self-denial. The more you express all of yourself, your pleasures as well as your abilities, the more formed a person you are. For us, discipline means organizing and orchestrating this panoply of inner resources so that it *coheres.* The task for us is not to repress part of the psyche, but to give the whole a shape. That is why we have become willing to submit more and more of the activities of our lives to formal training. We buy manuals on sex, assertiveness training, "hobby management" not because we are consumed by lust, rage, or frivolity, as the Victorians might have thought, but because we want to develop our capacities. Socially, this forming and training the whole self has a purpose. It makes you a person other people notice.

And here is where the subtlety of the chairman's speech begins. In his talk he makes what seems a flattering remark about how he would not understand the intricacies of what most of his manual laborers do. Their expertise arouses his respect; he recognizes their autonomy.

How likely would they be to believe him? His audience would, I think, accept the conclusion that autonomy and mutual recognition go hand in hand. They would doubt that they had developed themselves in any way to merit regard. In interviews which Jonathan Cobb and I conducted for the book

*The Hidden Injuries of Class,* we found that American workers harbor these doubts quite strongly. They attribute the fact that they do routine or manual jobs to their inability to "make something" of themselves, to "get themselves together." They believe they've failed to shape, to discipline themselves in the modern sense; the result is that they are "nobodies," or "just part of the woodwork." The families we interviewed attempt to compensate for their own sense of failure by rigidly controlling their children—this is particularly true of the working-class fathers. The children have no choice but to make more of themselves than their parents. An extraordinary novel by the English worker Robert Tressell, *The Ragged-Trousered Philanthropists,* conveys a similar divide between the ideal and oneself. The workers he observes are afraid to challenge their bosses because they think of themselves as bits and pieces of human beings who are not whole enough to be strong. They think, therefore, they deserve whatever they get. This view is shared by the American Teamsters Union official who tried to explain away the corruption in his union to a Senate committee by saying he represented simpleminded people who would not understand or expect anything better:

> We happen to be in a heavily and largely unskilled area . . . one does not have to have too many talents to drive a truck necessarily . . . most of us in our lifetimes have learned to drive an automobile.

Normal is unremarkable. Unremarkable is indistinguishable from others. No distinctions, nothing distinctive, no shape.

It seems an odd thing that the development of a coherent self should stigmatize other people, but this is precisely the social implication of autonomy. The chairman says he respects his employees for their autonomy. Let us then turn the statement around; if they are not autonomous, if they as sensible adults feel this, if he feels they are in fact not very distinctive, then he is not going to pay very much attention to them. The indifference which stigmatizes those who are perceived as lacking autonomy is equally expressed by statements of profound disregard like that made by the union official quoted above. A well-educated, self-assured person can take care of himself or herself, is independent, stands out from the crowd; all these images are expressed in the American slang that such persons have "class." They are the beacons. Images of those in the mass, by contrast, are of people whose characters are so unremarkable and underdeveloped as to arouse no interest. They are in shadow.

The surveys of occupational prestige in the United States, Italy, and Great Britain mentioned earlier show that this slang use of "class" is not accidental. In terms of occupation, relatively few people are perceived really to be autonomous. There is therefore an interesting connection between autonomy and other, deviant ways of standing out from a crowd. In his *Discipline and Punish,* Michel Foucault writes:

> In a system of discipline, the child is more individualized than the adult, the patient more than the healthy man, the madman and the delinquent more than the normal and the non-delinquent. In each case it is towards the first of these pairs that all the individualizing mechanisms are turned in our civilization; and when one wishes to individualize the healthy, normal and law-abiding adult, it is always by asking him how much of the child he has in him, what secret madness lies within him, what fundamental crime he has dreamt of committing.

Foucault's concept of individualism is of someone who is distinctive because he or she has a failing which is not "normal." Autonomy is about someone who has developed a talent, a personality, a style which is also not normal—but here the better word is "ordinary." For what "ordinary" implies is a state of being which is shapeless, unremarkable, bland—in a word, an amorphous condition of life.

A person who has marshalled his or her resources, who is therefore self-controlled—this autonomous figure can discipline others through making them feel ashamed. Indifference to ordinary people has, of course, a shaming effect: it makes them feel they don't count. The English industrialist put it succinctly in another part of his speech:

> We can't waste time in this company catering to everyone's whims. If we were not so hard pressed by our competitors I would make an effort, a great effort, to make this a place in which everyone has a task which best suits him. But I am hard pressed to keep us in business at all, and if you want special treatment as to tasks, overtime, and the like, you must step forward by virtue of your own achievements. Otherwise, you must accept things as they are decided by management.

But how does making other persons feel ashamed give one the consistent control over them implied in the term "discipline"? To understand this, it is necessary to understand how shame has become stronger as violence has waned in Western societies as an everyday tool of discipline.

I have sometimes wondered what it would be like for a modern person to be transported back to the life of an 18th Century household with servants, or to an early-19th Century factory: the shock of seeing domination expressed by the powerful in terms of bodily abuse of their servants or workers would be for us overwhelming. Servants in households of the old regime were routinely cuffed on the ears or kicked, women as well as men; in a 19th Century factory a foreman thought nothing of doing the same to a workman who was messing up on the job, and the worker, like the servant before him, thought nothing of it either. It was expected.

During the course of the 19th Century, the capacity of the powerful to deal out physical abuse changed somewhat in its terms. Breaking the skin—that is, breaking into the body of another person—was gradually seen as uncivilized. The whip, a common household utensil in the old regime for the discipline of both servants and children, was replaced by the paddle or *palmato* (a board with holes used throughout Southern Europe and the American South) to slap the palms of children; the violence adults inflicted on other adults came through the boot or the use of the hands. In the first English protests against caning in the 19th Century, reformers thought the practice in schools barbaric not so much because it caused great pain as because it was unsanitary; the wounds of a child who was caned easily became infected. Yet the association of power with the capacity to violate another person physically remained strong. On the streets of New York or Paris a century ago, a rich person in a carriage would hardly give a second thought to the matter if he splashed mire and mud from the road on a passerby. This was one of the original meanings of the American expression "being treated like dirt"; you were too poor to own a carriage, and had to walk.

In *The Civilizing Process,* Norbert Elias was the first to argue that shame became an increasingly important phenomenon in modern society as physical violence eroded. He notes, for instance, that the Victorians were ashamed of exposing themselves; women deformed the very shape of their bodies with corsets and stays, men neutralized their appearance through the ubiquitous black broadcloth suit which muffled the legs, arms, and chest in bags of nondescript material. He correlates this shame about the body to exposing the body of another person in order to inflict punishment; that also became uncomfortable. Although one could still feel easy baring the buttocks of a child about to be caned, one inflicted abuse on adults only on the exterior, as if, even though they were in one's power, one were embarrassed to see what was underneath. In some ways this explanation is unsatisfying. It ignores the political and ideological changes, beginning with Beccaria's *On Crimes and Punishments* in the 18th Century, which sought to express the dignity of man in terms of the sanctity of his body. But Elias's theory points also to a very important fact. The erosion of physical violation in the past century is not a sign of the lessening of coercion. It is a sign of a new set of controls like shame appearing, controls less palpable than physical pain but equal in their subduing effect.

Authority is an experience founded in part on the fear of a more powerful person, and the infliction of pain is a concrete basis for that power. Force might be defined in material terms other than sheer physical pain, of course. If you do not obey me, I will fire you. But this purely material answer is also losing its reality in modern society. You cannot fire me if I go on strike, either spontaneously or through my union; the laws of most Western countries protect my right to disobey you in this way. What then happens to authority when the punishment society allows is restricted—when neither the whip, starvation, nor the loss of a job is permitted?

Shame has taken the place of violence as a *routine* form of punishment in Western societies. The reason is simple and perverse. The shame an autonomous person can arouse in subordinates is an implicit control. Rather than the employer explicitly saying "You are dirt" or "Look how much better I am," all he needs to do is his job—exercise his skill or deploy his calm and indifference. His powers are fixed in his position, they are static attributes, qualities of what he is. It is not so much abrupt moments of humiliation as month after month of disregarding his employees, of not taking them seriously, which establishes his domination. The feelings he has about them, they about him, need never be stated. The grinding down of his employees' sense of self-worth is not part of his discourse with them; it is a silent erosion of their sense of self-worth which will wear them down. This, rather than open abuse, is how he bends them to his will. When shame is silent, implicit, it becomes a patent tool of bringing people to heel.

In totalitarian societies, the fear of violence makes the indifference of those in authority something ardently to be desired. A Czechoslovak colleague of mine tells the following story about herself, and it is worth quoting at length:

They had come to the office looking for dissident literature and she had shown them everything in her desk, everything in her purse. But she was not ironic in front of them. It was later, in describing the raid to a friend at a café, that she could permit herself to say that she had been honored with a visit from the state security police, but that she had, regrettably, been unable to assist them in the performance of their duties. She was no dissident. She could dimly remember the years before they came to power, but her parents remembered only too well; a black market for everything except the simplest food, furniture which had to be burned for heat during the worst days in winter. As an older girl she had lived on ration cards, but they were honored. At a certain point, however, she became aware of two facts. The first and simplest was that the dissidents disappeared. She lived in a modern state; that is, dissidents were rarely denounced in public; one day they would simply cease, like figures which are very real to us in a dream and then vanish with the light. The other fact was that the true believers in the regime, or those seeking special approval from it, were also in great danger. She remembered a boy at secretarial college who urged everyone to give up the meat ration cards for a week each month, so that food could be sent to the revolutionaries in Angola. He, too, ceased. Gradually she put these facts together.

To be unnoticeable is to survive. To wear one's normality as a mask, to long for the indifference of the authorities: this leads to the practice of a self-discipline far more rigid than anything the Victorians could have imagined. The most poignant example of totalitarian self-discipline I know is something a Soviet exile once told a researcher from Columbia University about forcing himself to smoke a pipe:

> While smoking a pipe the face does not reveal so much. See, this we learned during the Soviet period. Before the revolutions we used to say: "The eyes are the mirror of the soul." The eyes can lie—and how. You can express with your eyes a devoted attention which in reality you are not feeling. You can express serenity or surprise. It is much more difficult to govern the expression of your mouth. I often watch my face in the mirror before going to meetings and demonstrations and I saw . . . I was suddenly aware that even with a memory of a disappointment my lips became closed. That is why by smoking a heavy pipe you are more sure of yourself. Through the heaviness of the pipe the lips are deformed and cannot react spontaneously.

Everything is different for us: the definition of force, punishment, discipline. Our first thought is not "How can I disguise myself?" when we move to a new community. Nor need we discreetly try out signals of individual taste, feeling, and perception, so that after a few months we feel we can trust one another and remove the veil of neutrality. This whole way of surviving hasn't as much weight in our lives as does something which our very freedom makes possible, and makes a problem. The pressure on us is detachment from a condition which seems shameful, the condition of unnoticeability. I suppose that a desire for special treatment, viewed from the perspective of this Russian, would be an act of sheer folly. But it is, from our vantage point, not folly but an attempt to gain what is in advanced capitalist society in short supply: a sense of respect and recognition from others in going about the ordinary business of living, and in being just an ordinary person. Self-declaration has for us a moral weight, and being noticed has a meaning in terms of social hierarchy. It is our attempt to break the disciplinary bond, a bond in which our inferiority makes us not worth noticing.

I want now to show how the practice of complex autonomy can nonetheless create a bond between superior and subordinate. It is a bond in which the subordinate feels a sense of dread about the attitudes of autonomy evinced by his superior, feels that mixture of fear and awe which is the most essential ingredient of authority. In the particular case study materials I shall use, there does come a moment of breaking the pattern of discipline. The subordinate reacts explosively against his superior, but in the process becomes more and more dependent. The case recalls the pattern of Miss Bowen's disobedient dependence. It also sets out concretely assumptions made in modern bureaucratic ideologies about how autonomous figures of authority ought to manipulate others to reestablish disciplinary control.


## THE BOND AUTONOMY CREATES

The following case study appeared in the *Harvard Business Review* in June 1965. It has often been cited in management circles as a model of how an employer should deal with a demanding employee.

Dr. Richard Dodds, a physics research worker, entered the office and showed his superior, Dr. Blackman, a letter. This letter was from another research institution, offering Dodds a position. Blackman read the letter.

Dodds: "What do you think of that?"

Blackman: "I knew it was coming. He asked me if it would be all right if he sent it. I told him to go ahead, if he wanted to."

Dodds: "I didn't expect it, particularly after what you said to me last time [pause]. I'm really quite happy here. I don't want you to get the idea that I am thinking of leaving. But I thought I should go and visit him—I think he expects it—and I wanted to let you know that just because I was thinking of going down, that didn't mean I was thinking of leaving here, unless of course, he offers me something extraordinary."

Blackman: "Why are you telling me all this?"

Dodds: "Because I didn't want you hearing from somebody else that I'm thinking of leaving here because I was going for a visit to another institution. I really have no intention of leaving here, you know, unless he offers me something really extraordinary that I can't afford to turn down. I think I'll tell him that, that I am willing to look at his laboratory, but unless there is something unusual for me, I have no intention of leaving here."

Blackman: "It's up to you."

Dodds: "What do you think?"

Blackman: "Well, what? About what? You've got to make up your own mind."

Dodds: "I don't consider too seriously this job. He is not offering anything really extraordinary. But I am interested in what he had to say, I would like to look around his lab."

Blackman: "Sooner or later you are going to have to make up your mind where you want to work."

Dodds replied sharply: "That depends on the offers, doesn't it?"

Blackman: "No, not really; a good man always gets offers. You get a good offer and you move, and as soon as you have moved, you get other good offers. It would throw you into confusion to consider all the good offers you will receive. Isn't there a factor of how stable you want to be?"

Dodds: "But I'm not shopping around. I already told you that. He sent me this letter, I didn't ask him to. All I said was that I should visit him, and to you that's shopping around."

Blackman: "Well, you may choose to set aside your commitment here if he offers you something better. All I am saying is that you will still be left with the question of you've got to stay some place, and where is that going to be?"

The discussion continued on how it would look if Dodds changed jobs at this point, and finally Dodds said:

Dodds: "Look, I came in here, and I want to be honest with you, but you go and make me feel guilty, and I don't like that."

Blackman: "You are being honest as can be."

Dodds: "I didn't come in here to fight. I don't want to disturb you."

Blackman: "I'm not disturbed. If you think it is best for you to go somewhere else, that is O.K. with me."

Again there is a lengthy exchange about what does Dodds really want and how would his leaving look to others. Finally Dodds blurts out:

Dodds: "I don't understand you. I came in here to be honest with you, and you make me feel guilty. All I wanted was to show you this letter, and let you know what I was going to do. What should I have told you?"

Blackman: "That you had read the letter, and felt that under the circumstances it was necessary for you to pay a visit to the professor, but that you were happy here, and wanted to stay at least until you had got a job of work done."

Dodds: "I can't get over it. You think there isn't a place in the world I'd rather be than here in this lab. . . ."

The purpose of the discussion seems simple. A man reports to his boss that he has been offered the possibility of another job. In the back of his mind, quite probably, he is hoping the boss will say that whatever outside offer the man receives his current company will match. As the discussion proceeds, however, the boss responds in such a way that the man feels disloyal and guilty about even considering leaving. By the end of the interview, Dr. Dodds is in no shape emotionally to make a hardheaded decision about his own career.

There is one way in which his employer is reminiscent of

George Pullman. When Dr. Dodds first mentions the letter, Blackman responds: "I knew it was coming. He asked me if it would be all right if he sent it. I told him to go ahead, if he wanted to." Blackman has in effect approved the offer from the outside; it is because of him that the employee has any good fortune at all.

The superior controls reality. Psychological as well as material reality. In the middle of their discussion Dodds says that Blackman is making him feel guilty, to which Blackman replies, "You are being as honest as can be." When one person says I feel guilty and the other responds you are being as honest as you can, they are talking on two different emotional planes. The first, the subordinate's, is about the emotions a particular discussion arouses in him; the second, the superior's, is a judgement of the whole moral character of the discussant. This judgement on the surface seems a compliment. But the approval of someone who sees beyond the moment, to make a total judgement of another person, has a cowing and subduing effect. This effect appears directly in the subordinate's next sentences: "I didn't come in here to fight. I don't want to disturb you."

Pullman controlled the total reality of his employees, their housing, smoking, socializing, as well as their jobs; he thought he could control these experiences better than the employees could for themselves. In the exchanges between Dodds and Blackman, the boss also conveys that he sees and controls a reality the subordinate cannot: literally, in having authorized the job offer; psychologically, in responding to specific feelings of the subordinate by making judgements on his whole character.

There is a gulf, however, between the old-style paternalistic boss and this employer. Everything Pullman did called attention to himself; every employee in the town should know who was personally the cause of his or her well-being. In the interview between Dodds and Blackman, the employer does not draw attention to himself. He consistently focuses the employee back upon his own responses, aspirations, and feelings.

The employer avoids dealing with his employee person-to-person through a technique I shall call reversed responses.

Reversed responses begin almost as soon as the discussion opens. Dodds says he is happy in his present job, but would leave for an extraordinary offer. Blackman, instead of responding in any direct way, such as "Of course," or "Don't go" or "What do you mean by 'extraordinary,'" replies: "Why are you telling me all this?" throwing the entire burden of the conversation back on the employee to justify himself. Dodds reacts by trying to do so. He says: "Because I didn't want you hearing from someone else that I was thinking of leaving here because I was going for a visit to another institution." They are both now talking on the superior's terms. The superior is in control by evading a direct reply; i.e., that he could or will make Dodds a counter-offer. Instead, they are discussing whether Dodds is loyal.

The reversed responses appear whenever the superior is called on or challenged. When Dodds reiterates his statement that he will leave only if a better job is offered him, Blackman replies, "It's up to you"; later, when Dodds says pathetically, "I don't want to disturb you," his employer gives the ultimate in a neutral, non-personal reply: "I'm not disturbed. If you think it is best for you to go somewhere else, that is O.K. with me."

We might be tempted to say that here is the perfect example of bureaucratic impersonality—except that the subordinate feels these reversed responses deeply. The more Dodds enters into this discussion, the more personally upset he becomes—at this counselor who always focuses the issue back on his own choice and feelings, who never declares himself really involved. Because the boss gives nothing of himself, it is the employee who is conducting his own loyalty test—with the boss's helpful "We were discussing you, not me."

Reversed responses have their strongest emotional impact on the very concept of discourse. They tend to discredit the statements of the other party as intrinsically meaningful. When a superior says of an employee's professional prospects

"Why are you telling me all this?"—in defiance of the obvious reasons why—the employee is being told that his intentions are not revealed by what he states directly: something hidden must be the real meaning. The whole of Blackman's discussion is conducted this way. The employer is helping the employee get at something the employee does not understand about himself. By refusing to credit the discourse of a subordinate as having an intrinsic meaning, Blackman can eventually focus Dodds on his feelings divorced from his professional situation: they become intensely disturbing, yet in limbo. As a result, Dodds feels more and more out of control; he does not press his employer to match the outside job; he appeals to his employer to tell him how he ought to have acted in announcing he received a letter the employer already knew about.

Reversing response as this employer does serves several purposes. First of all, a struggle for recognition is set up. The employee wants his boss to respond in kind to his problem— he may change jobs—and the boss does not respond by discussing how work at the present job is in fact better than the new prospect or by making a counter-offer. Instead, the boss establishes his own dominance by the practice of indifference. "If you think it is best for you to go somewhere else, that is O.K. with me." An odd statement for a man who has shortly before told the same employee that he is so talented he is likely to receive many offers in the future. As the employee becomes more upset, the boss keeps his cool. Keeping calm in the face of someone else's anger is always a way to stay in control in a conflict. But here a conversation which began amicably becomes heated on one side precisely because there is no response in kind on the other. Moreover, the employee shows signs of becoming emotionally dependent on the employer by the very process of reversing response. The moment is extraordinary:

"I don't understand you. I came in here to be honest with you, and you make me feel guilty. All I wanted was to show you this letter, and let you know what I was going to do. What should I have told you?"

The boss proceeds to tell him how he could have acted better. If he had acted better, he wouldn't be so upset. The boss acts indifferent to the fact, as the employee tells him so graphically, that something in his own behavior has upset the employee. Instead he is teaching the employee how to understand himself more fully.

The result of this process echoes Foucault's idea that "When one wishes to individualize the healthy, normal, and law-abiding adult, it is always by asking him how much of the child he has in him, what secret madness lies within him. . . ." This calm employer has elicited infantile rage from his employee simply by remaining, on the surface, cool and adult. What's wrong with you? That question is individualizing; you focus on yourself to explain, to justify. Conversely, the employer has revealed nothing of himself: he does not respond to influences; he exerts them. This imbalance is his autonomy.

The bond between these two is forged from this imbalance. When Dodds first asks, Will you make it worth my while to remain here, Blackman replies by saying, You have a problem in being loyal because of the kind of person you are—unstable, grasping at opportunities, and the like. When the reversed response takes hold, the subordinate asks himself, Am I a loyal person?, not Are this man and this job worthy of my loyalty?

In the disobedient dependence of Miss Bowen, the knot between her and her father strengthened when she transgressed his desires. In the interview between Dodds and Blackman, the subordinate becomes angry at his employer for doubting his loyalty, in fact ends the interview with a declaration of disloyalty—"You think there isn't a place in the world I'd rather be than here in this lab"—and is emotionally in his employer's grip. He is bidding for recognition; he wants to shake his superior out of indifference, to be seen as a person by his employer. This play between recognition and indifference is how the knot tightens. The superior remains in control of the apparatus of recognition; his or her attention is the prize of disruption. In this framework, negation is no step to freedom. I once showed my Czechoslovak colleague the transcript of the interview between Dodds and Blackman, and asked her what she made of the employer's canny statements of, Do what you want, I don't care. "It seems to me all such a luxury," she replied, "but then, I never met a man who needed to play such games."

It would be wrong to look at the employer as consciously Machiavellian. Blackman would have to be a great actor to contrive and execute such an interview. He is instead playing according to a set of rules, following a set of assumptions, about how to deal with threats from below. These assumptions are that something other than threats will be more effective; in any event, here—unlike in the 18th Century factory, physical abuse is out of the question. The rules he follows are the same as those which lead people to idealize doctors or research scientists as "higher" in society than the managers of large corporations. They are the same rules which make workers feel ambivalent about expressing their demands out of the conviction that their inner lives are less developed than those of their betters. The employer is exerting influence as a figure of autonomous authority, influence which binds his disobedient employee to him as a potent figure whose recognition must be won.

In the preceding chapter we spoke of paternalism as a false profession of care. Here we must understand autonomy as involving another kind of illusion: a disguise of power, so that it seems to come from nowhere, to be impersonal, a disguise embodied in the very word "influence."

## INFLUENCE

To understand this disguise, we need first to take note of an important historical fact. In the old regime, how the masses of people survived was thought to have very little to do with the principles and persons of authority. Work was thought akin to the life of beasts. Montesquieu does not frame his principles of just and unjust authority according to the work people do, nor even did Rousseau. In the letters of Madame de Sévigné, labor is invisible. It was Diderot's great *Encyclopedia*, published toward the close of the 18th Century, in which the awareness of work dawned as important for a more general understanding of society, and it is the writings of Marx and Engels which brought this awareness to fruition. How people are conscious of their work, their bosses, and themselves is the basis of authority in society.

The ideologies of paternalism in the 19th Century were one acknowledgement of the need to justify hard work to those who were laboring for others. By the First World War, this justification was beginning to wear thin, as was the promise of the market ideology itself to include more and more individuals among its beneficiaries. The problem could be measured. In the 1920's, American, German, and British employers began to take the sort of statistics which showed that the productivity of their workers was declining compared to the productivity of workers a generation before. Appeals to the glories of market competition did not seem to be of much help, nor did professions of a desire to take good care of employees.

By now a great deal is known about the relation of worker motivation to productivity. The relation is not a direct, positive correlation. For instance, a study conducted in American factories after the Second World War found that alienated workers can be highly productive; they simply do their jobs without thinking about them, getting through the day with as little fuss as possible because they feel so disconnected. It is also known that there are many work situations in which workers become less productive when they get interested in the work; they savor the tasks they do, and so do them slowly, or they begin asking questions about why the work is organized one way or another rather than just taking orders.

Motivation fluctuates over time as well; it depends upon a

complex set of economic, demographic, and cultural factors. At the present moment, North American and many European countries are experiencing a "crisis" in worker motivation comparable to that which appeared in the 1920's. Signs of sheer discontent have been deftly characterized in a book by Robert S. Gilmour and Robert G. Lamb, *Political Alienation in Contemporary America,* who have uncovered some startling statistics about the discontents workers feel about their work, and the suspicions they harbor about their bosses. While less than a tenth of the professionals in their study were highly disaffected and suspicious, 40 percent of the service workers and a third of the industrial operatives felt so. These latter two categories from the great bulk of workers in industrial society. People who are disaffected can express themselves in a number of ways. Workers who are dissatisfied with the chain of command and obedience in which they labor are resisting established power in ways which, increasingly, have little to do with organized protest. Unions, now themselves large bureaucracies, are more and more seen as distant organizations that collaborate with the enemy. Disaffection appears in more spontaneous, isolated, perhaps pathetic ways which interfere with productivity.

For instance, voluntary absenteeism has become a major worry for both public and private bureaucracies. It involves not only feigning sickness to take paid sick leave; absenteeism also involves at the white-collar level people simply disappearing for the day or lying about things they need to do outside the office. As the scale of the phenomenon has grown, the perception of it has changed. Personnel experts no longer regard it as simple delinquency; they now see it as a tactic of resistance. In the last decade, also, the volume of wildcat strikes has risen, strikes as much—as in the cases of the United Mine Workers and the British auto workers—against the union leadership as against the managerial bureaucracy. These breaks in "worker discipline," as the socialists used to describe them, are appearing in England, Italy, and France, as well as in North America.

The reason such discontents are related to authority has to do with the fact that now the *quality* of work experience is at issue. At the heart of this experience is the human relationship between workers and bosses. A recent study of dissatisfactions among Italian office workers lists the following complaints, in decreasing order of frequency: bosses do not protect us as much as they should from outside pressures; bosses do not divide up work fairly; bosses fail to take initiative; there is too much needless repetition of activity in the office; paperwork is meaningless; the pay is too low for the difficulty of the work involved. A study in progress of printers in Germany lists so far the following complaints, again in decreasing order of frequency: bosses are too indecisive, there is not enough variety of tasks; bosses are unconcerned about the quality of the product; there is too much bureaucratic infighting; social-service benefits are too low; there are too many jealous people in the shop. American studies emphasize more the matter of personal satisfaction in the relations between bosses and their employees. English and French studies of worker attitudes reveal the most economically oriented consciousness, but even in these instances the boss as a person tends to be held personally responsible for the material deprivations his charges experience.

The quality of work life was a secondary issue in societies of severe economic misery for the masses, like England in the middle of the 19th Century, or societies with many good jobs but many more people who wanted to work, like the United States at the same time. One puts up with employers who are inept, fools, or unpleasant if one wants to eat. Modern industrial society has lightened the material hardships of the masses, and made working a more stable and regular experience; now it becomes possible to think about the quality of what one does during those eight hours. When a recent study by the American government—larger in scale but less careful than Gilmour and Lamb's—revealed that a majority of workers in non-élite jobs were profoundly unsatisfied about the way they spent their time working, a prominent businessman remarked that the government had studied the ultimate luxury, the luxury of enjoying what one does. This remark misses both the historical and the practical point. By a terrible irony, modern capitalism has come to give workers the material opportunity to confront what it means to be tense or bored during the major part of one's waking hours. The practical result of this confrontation is that the productivity and the discipline of the system are disturbed by such acts as voluntary absenteeism or wildcat strikes.

One way the discontents with work now have been explained is the assertion that the "work ethic" is breaking down. This assertion is based on another notion of Max Weber's, an idea that people want to work hard, no matter how oppressed they are in the process, because the self-discipline involved gives them a sense of moral worth. This is what the Protestant ethic means for people who are not capitalists. The assertion that this ethic is breaking down, in the abstract, is simply not true. There are a number of studies which show that people of all ages, races, and classes still claim to believe in the inherent moral value of hard work. The meaning of this morality, however, is changing. Hard work is coming to be seen by many workers as a means to another end, that of personal development, rather than as morally worthwhile in itself.

In an interesting article in a volume of essays, *Work in America,* Daniel Yankelovich precisely connects this new morality to workers' perceptions of the authority of their bosses. His argument is that a worker does not feel his interests or perceptiveness develop in the abstract; these experiences while processing papers or making machines are related in the worker's mind to what kind of boss the worker has. Basing this assertion on a variety of studies, including his own surveys, Yankelovich concludes:

[The new breed of workers] often start a job willing to work hard and be productive. But if the job fails to meet their expectations —if it doesn't give them the incentive they are looking for—then they lose interest. They may use the job to satisfy their own needs but give little in return. The preoccupation with self that is the hallmark of New Breed values places the burden of providing [emotional] incentives for hard work more squarely on the employer than under the old value system.

This is the conundrum of work: if it is to be qualitatively, emotionally satisfying, as more and more workers want, then the personality of the boss becomes especially important. He gives the work part of that emotional meaning by being a person worth working for. This is how personality and office become joined. A classical Marxist would say a boss never could be satisfactory on these terms; the new element is what workers feel the bosses ought to be.

It is for these reasons that, from the 1920's on, managers have been turning to psychology and psychologists to find new ways to motivate employees unmoved by the shibboleths of high capitalism. The most famous of these psychologists was Frederick Winslow Taylor, a behaviorist who owed his ideas to the work of Pavlov and Watson. Taylor set about to design work "scientifically" so that productivity could be increased by a carefully chosen set of rewards. The Taylorite movement was responsible for broadening the horizons of American business schools, which previously had only taught such technical subjects as accounting and investment, and for broadening the work of continental institutions like the École Nationale d'Administration in France, which had previously focused on governmental policy and procedure. Although the scientific pretensions of the Taylorite movement have largely been discredited, its strategic goals have become ever more pervasive in the training of managers and in managerial practices.

The most important goal is to create a new image of the authority of employers. This image is based not on threatening the employee but rather on psychologically gratifying the employee. The employer appears as the "facilitator" of impersonal policy, the "coordinator" of work tasks, and so on; he influences rather than orders. In an essay written years ago,

"Work and Its Discontents," Daniel Bell aptly characterized this change:

> . . . in the evident concern with understanding, communication, and participation, we find a change in the outlook of management, parallel to that which is occurring in the culture as a whole from authority to manipulation as a means of exercising domination. The ends of the enterprise remain, but the means have shifted, and the older modes of overt coercion are now replaced by psychological persuasion. The tough brutal foreman, raucously giving orders, gives way to the mellowed voice of the "human relations oriented" supervisor.

The attempts to redefine the images of work and of employers echo the relation of Dodds and Blackman on an enlarged scale. The new ideology of work focuses on what the worker feels; what he or she is capable of feeling is a matter of internal development and discipline; the boss as an influence disappears as a person. The influence seems to come from nowhere, but the employee is strongly moved.

There are now established three schools of thought about the psychological influencing of employees. The first approach is the most obvious. It attempts to make work intrinsically satisfying; the employer simply hopes that someone happy in a job will do it well. Administrators concerned with making work satisfying have in the past experimented with variable-speed assembly lines in American electronics plants, so that manual laborers can go at their own pace; with job rotation at the Volvo auto works in Sweden, so that both manual and white-collar workers are relieved of monotony by working through a series of tasks. Job-contentment experts also tinker with such matters as how to light an office or when to pipe canned music into a shop. Recently, however, their advice has become more spiritual: they speak of "self-realization" on the assembly line, the canteen as an "intimacy forum."

The second school is based on what the trade calls "Theory X." It is Skinnerian psychology applied to industrial management. According to this school, managers should not worry about the intrinsic satisfactions of a job; rather, they should design rewards in recognition for doing the work well. If a worker does his work poorly, his punishment should be simply to be ignored. Theory X is founded on a rather glum view of human nature: human beings are not very much concerned with the quality of their experiences at work. As a sensible critic of Skinnerian management, Douglas McGregor has observed that the practitioners of Theory X are further convinced that since most people are inherently weak or stupid, their capacity to reap rewards is limited, no matter how much they may want them. Thus, the practitioner of Theory X has to create a set of rewards which the "normal" labor market will not provide for the masses. The obvious thing administrators adhering to this view have done in the past is increase wages during the days or hours a worker is especially productive. But this creates so much resentment among other workers that it is counter-productive. The proponents of Theory X have therefore had to seek out less obvious rewards. For instance, they have experimented with such concepts as "reward clocks"; if a worker does a job in five minutes which normally takes ten, he gets five minutes of paid rest; if he does the job in three minutes, he gets a bonus—eight rather than seven minutes of paid rest—and so on.

The third school is currently the most fashionable. It emphasizes the idea of cooperation. Tangible industrial results like productivity, this school maintains, depend on the process by which goals are set and tasks defined. When workers participate in these decisions, they will work hard, even if the work is intrinsically not to their taste, and even if the extrinsic rewards are not great. The reason they will do so is that they have come to feel responsible for what they are doing. The practices of this school are trapped in capitalist realities, however. Corporations engage in cooperative practices because they see them as a means to an end like greater productivity. By contrast, truly socialist experiments in worker cooperation, as the Yugoslav sociologist Rudi Supek has pointed out, treat cooperation as an important end in itself, one for which productivity may be sacrificed. Moreover, corporate cooperation takes place among unequals. The experiments in cooperative decision-making make use of employee questionnaires to find out how workers want to do a job, or they make use of conferences with workers at the job site. These techniques try to create a feeling of mutuality and hence of good will between those who, in the end, will influence and those who will be influenced.

The psychological aim of all three approaches is one of stimulation, not autonomy for the worker himself. Those who emphasize job satisfaction seldom think of the worker designing the tasks that would most interest him: it would be a massively expensive endeavor, with no guarantee that the worker would design for himself a job of use to the bureaucracy. The possibilities of work are defined by the authorities; they decide what the worker would most likely be interested in by using tests and interviews. The Theory X people don't let the worker have much of a voice in setting the terms of his own conditioning; the rewards and punishments are set for him because the Theory X people assume no one would "play fair" by assigning real punishments for himself. The realities of control in the third, "cooperative school" have been rather ruefully described by a psychologist working for a large chemical firm:

> Too often we ask for employees' attitudes and opinions in great detail, but in most cases, once we have the data, nothing is done with it. And this is because the employees are telling management what it doesn't want to hear, so management ignores the findings. Then they wonder why we continue to have discontent, grievances, and strikes. It would be better not to ask the employees what they believe and feel than to ask them and do nothing.

Each of these approaches has met with mixed success. But despite their ambiguous efficacy, these efforts are pursued because they are a way to give a human *raison d'être* to corporate life. The essence of this humanizing is to disguise the sheer fact of command. The reason employees should work in a hierarchical structure is, ultimately, their own happiness. Power is conceived as the capacity to influence another person in ways that a person will ultimately find gratifying. Employees, the objects of power, are minutely analyzed to see how they can be influenced; the subject doing the influencing is treated as neutral. Dr. Dodds's employer is such an influence.

The most graphic rationale of this concept of influence appears in the work of Herbert Simon, the founding father of administrative science. The major works of Herbert Simon are *Administrative Behavior* and *Models of Man.* In these books, he is concerned to show that corporations make decisions not only according to external market conditions but also according to how the corporation is internally organized. This internal organization he conceives of as a network of influences, the influence of each person determined by his position and function in the corporation. The concept of influence in the work of Herbert Simon is morally chaste; manipulation, deception, and self-protection seem to play a negligible part in the process of influencing others and so arriving at decisions. Influence, as portrayed in these influential works, has the same relation to the struggle for existence in corporations as Henri Murger's *La Vie de Bohème* had to the actual life of the poor in 19th Century Paris.

The subject that has fascinated Simon throughout his career is how to build "models" of the influences within an organization. One would suppose that the patterns of influence ought to have something to do with the tasks which an organization must perform, and that therefore a model of administrative behavior ought to be linked to the problems a corporation faces when it tries to increase its economic power and make money. In Simon's work, however, the corporation is a world unto itself. He has attempted to divorce the way decisions are made from the nature of decisions to be made about competition, capital expansion, merger, and the like. The attempt is not irrational. His original purpose was to show that bureaucratic activity within corporations is not simply a matter of responding to external market influences. While a corporation might on paper be arranged as a neat chain of command, in actual practice a corporation is a maze of lines of communication, with most people subject to many conflicting pressures. The problem with the seemingly sensible position is that Simon has gone to the extreme in trying to avoid the mistake of viewing corporate decision-making as market-determined. He has cut the corporation off from the outside world. This way influence is never blemished by the hard realities of life.

This concept of influence, whatever its intellectual defects, reveals a basic attitude about authority on the part of administrators and administrative scientists. If authority in general is a meaning people ascribe to acts of command-and-obedience, in this scheme of things authority has every possible meaning all at once, and therefore no meaning at all. Here, for example, is how a popular textbook for business students, *Effective Managerial Leadership,* by James J. Cribbin, defines a good, "collaborative" manager:

He does not hesitate to be forceful when circumstances require, but he does not resort to directiveness as a matter of course. He prizes self-discipline over imposed discipline and constructive suggestions over submissive conformity. Viewing authority as based on competence rather than position, this leader interacts with his followers in a process of mutual influence. As a team builder, he realizes that his objective is to help employees satisfy some of their needs while achieving the goals of the group and the firm. Communication is free flowing, constructive, and directed to the purposes for which the group exists. Finally, if possible, conflict is resolved by the synthesis of diverse views.

Since "influence" is a self-contained, self-referring system, the good manager must be everywhere and everything. Since "influence" is morally chaste, everywhere and everything he is ought to be for the good of those he influences. At a seemingly higher level, this same notion of influence as a free-floating phenomenon appears in the work of Chris Argyris, a Professor of Industrial Administration at Yale:

It is, therefore, the responsibility of every executive in the organization that is considering any of these major organizational changes to develop first his competence in several leadership patterns so that he is able to shift from one to another with minimal ambiguity and personal insecurity. The leader will need to have this philosophy of leadership fully internalized. An operational criterion of adequate internalization is that his confidence in the reality-centered leadership is so high that he will not tend to feel insecure or guilty when and if he is questioned about his changing behavior from, for example, being directive to becoming more participative.

The point of these ideologies of influence is that the effective manager is never tied down, never committed. And this is precisely how he or she maintains autonomy. The expertise of a "coordinator" or a "facilitator" is never to be caught in a position. This is what Dr. Dodds's employer practices so successfully; his reversed responses keep him free of having to commit himself about how he will meet the outside company's offer. He will probably do so only after he has met in a personnel committee, like the one the accountants' boss belongs to, and so the ultimate decision will be even further away from being his personal decision. We commonly think of good managers as decisive; the truly effective manager, on the contrary, covers his flanks. There are many polite ways to say this: he keeps his lines of influence open, he is flexible, or, in Argyris's trenchant phrase, he is able to shift positions "with minimal ambiguity and personal insecurity."

The idea of influence is thus the ultimate expression of autonomy. Its effect is to mystify what the boss wants and what the boss stands for. Influence directed to making workers more content with their work denies them a similar freedom; the nature of the contentments is designed for them. Pleasure is expected to erase confrontation. However, the influencers do not say who they are, what they stand for, or what they expect; the influences are not rules but stimulations. It is up to the subordinate to find the design. This is the most extreme example of a saying of

Hegel's: the injustice of society is that the subordinate must make sense of what power is.

## AUTONOMY AND FREEDOM

One of the reasons autonomy elicits such strong feelings is that many people have come to believe that to be autonomous is to be free. "As long as you can be pushed around," a laborer in Boston once told me, "you are nothing." In the minds of ordinary people, to control the flow of influence brings not so much the pleasures of domination but a chance to get in control of oneself. Autonomy builds a barrier against the world; once shielded, a person can live as he or she wants.

Tocqueville, in the second volume of his *Democracy in America,* was the first to write about the belief in autonomy as freedom, and this theme is one reason his description of Jacksonian America speaks to the modern reader not as a portrait of a past age but of the present age in germ. Tocqueville uses the terminology of his time to describe this belief; he speaks of freedom as the goal of "individualism"—but by individualism he intends something unlike what his contemporaries understood the word to mean. In the opening of the second part of volume two of the *Democracy,* Tocqueville draws a famous contrast between individualism and egoism, for example. Egoism is

> a passionate and exaggerated love of oneself, which leads a person to relate everything to himself and to prefer his own needs to everything else.

Individualism is

> a peaceful and moderated feeling, which leads each citizen to isolate himself from the mass of his equals and to withdraw within the circle of his family and his friends. Further, having created this little society for his immediate ease, he willingly abandons the larger society to go its own way.

This is not the individualism of the Social Darwinists, not a force of rugged struggle for survival, agonistic and hard; just the reverse. It is not the individualism Jacob Burckhardt imagined born in the Italian Renaissance, growing ever stronger in modern history. Burckhardt shows us men and women struggling to win praise from each other, struggling to be recognized as individuals because they have special qualities. This display of *virtus* involves a strong sense of community, of wanting to make contact with others. Tocqueville shows us men and women whose desire is rather to be left alone. Neither avaricious entrepreneurs nor forceful characters seeking applause, they want to be left to themselves so that they can develop their interests, their tastes, their intimate feelings.

It is a compassionate picture that Tocqueville paints of these individualists, a picture of the softer impulses of ordinary people. But these dreams of individual development will shatter if there is anyone stronger invading the sacred space of the self, like a loud noise from the street which prevents one from pursuing a train of thought in one's own mind. And thus a very strong desire comes over this individual. It is first of all to equalize the condition of power in society so that no one has the strength to intrude; if all are equal, all can go their separate ways. Tocqueville describes this as the principle of "democratic individualism," using in this phrase "democratic" to mean "equal," as Tocqueville's American biographer, George Pierson, remarks.

But if social conditions do not permit people to be equal, there is a second line of defense. It is indifference, withdrawal, a willful numbness to others. If you act this way, they can't get at you emotionally. A prisoner in the world, you can nonetheless go your own way inside. It is this second line of defense which embodies autonomy as an ideal of freedom in the lives of those who are dependent upon others.

The whole of the second volume of Tocqueville's *Democracy* is devoted to understanding the tragic consequences of this ideal. These consequences are both psychological and political. The psychological consequence is that one is endlessly looking inside for a sense of fulfillment, as though the self were like a vast warehouse of gratification that one's social relations had kept one from exploring:

> Independent of whatever a person experiences at a given moment he imagines a thousand other gratifications which death will keep him from knowing, if he does not hurry. The thought troubles him, fills him with fear and regret, and maintains his spirit in a state of incessant trepidation; at every moment he feels he is on the verge of changing his designs and his place in life.

Isolated, restless, and unfulfilled: to look for freedom through autonomy creates a terrible anxiety.

The political consequences of this ideal are equally destructive. As the second line of defense against intrusion from the outside is treating power at arm's length, something one can't let matter, one becomes willing to surrender more and more legal rights to the state, to give it more and more scope, if only it doesn't press too hard on intimate life. A state which would meet these conditions would be "absolute, highly articulate, regular, farseeing and soft." I believe Tocqueville is the first writer to use the term "welfare statism," and here is his picture of it:

> What I reproach equality for is not that it leads men astray in the pursuit of forbidden pleasure but rather absorbs them wholly in the pursuit of those pleasures which are allowed ... it is likely that a kind of well-meaning materialism [*matérialisme honnête*] is going to be established in the world, one which will not corrupt the soul but noiselessly unbend its springs of action.

These are the psychological and political reasons why Tocqueville feared the belief that people are free when they are autonomous. The belief will make them endlessly unsatisfied and may accustom them to the ways of a soft and enervating state. And in this second volume of the *Democracy* Tocqueville is at his least conservative; the answer to this belief is not aggressive, competitive individualism but more sociable ideas of freedom.

The fear Tocqueville had was that the ideal of being free through being autonomous would be so compelling that these dangers would be overlooked until it was too late. It is true that the belief in autonomy has come to be widespread, if surveys of occupational status and desirable personality traits are a good guide. It is true that the value placed on autonomy by those who lack it can reinforce the authority of those who are perceived to possess it. The possessors are higher, freer; autonomy is a way to conceive of what it is to be a strong person. But what Tocqueville feared has to be set in a broader context, the relation between authority and freedom as Western industrial society now knows it.

We have a freedom to disbelieve in authority, and more importantly to declare our disbelief, a freedom unknown in the various fatherlands. The dominant images of authority invite these rejections. At one pole is the image of paternalistic authority in which there is something indelibly and glaringly false: it is concern on the master's part when it suits his interests, on his terms, and at the price of the grateful passivity of the recipients. At the other pole is an image shorn of any profession of "Let me take care of you." It is the image of a person who takes care of himself. He shows his self-possession by acts of indifference or withdrawal from others—a process mistakenly labeled "impersonal behavior," since it elicits the most intensely personal feelings of rejection on the part of those who are subject to it. The source of these rejections, a concrete person who is responsible to others and must deal with them person-to-person, is becoming more and more veiled in modern bureaucratic practice as the authorities become the shapers of influence rather than overt figures with power. An authoritative presence, then, without responsibilities, a dealer in influence who does not deal face-to-face. A judge whose verdicts are both intense and arbitrary: matters of regard. And this, too, makes him free.

These images of authority developed out of basic ambiguities in capitalism, ambiguities in the meaning of community and individualism. Neither image of authority succeeded in banishing these ambiguities permanently, and that failure also has kept us free. The Führer and the Duce are two sharp lessons in what European society would look like if the dissonances were to disappear.

Our problem is a problem within the domain of being free, and it is a real problem. The dominant forms of authority in our lives are destructive; they lack nurturance, nurturance—the love which sustains others—is a basic human need, as basic as eating or sex. Compassion, trust, reassurance are qualities it would be absurd to associate with these figures of authority in the adult world. And yet we are free: free to accuse our masters that these qualities are missing.

The difficulty is that the very act of rejecting them builds bonds with them. Bonds based on fear of their strength, or the desire to glimpse some image of strength through defining their failings, attempts to wrest from an unsatisfying set of images something which will satisfy that basic need for authority. Because of the seriousness of the authority's trade, he is a mesmerizing figure. One may be disloyal to him, one may transgress him, but, as it was for Dr. Dodds or Miss Bowen, the purpose of these negations is not to dethrone the authoritative presence but to attract notice.

Surely a person with any sense would resent being in the hands of these elusive or deceiving authorities. But the trap of rejecting them is more than a matter of hoping finally to get them to care. No one person, no matter how well-meaning as a personality, can ever give nurturance to another person as though it were a commodity. Nor do you earn care as though earning interest on an investment. But the illusion protects itself. The person who is unsatisfied, unhappy imagines that if only there were someone different in control, then the unhappiness would end, one would feel respected by being noticed. Dr. Dodds imagines a different kind of boss would have made him feel less guilty; it is not how he and his employer talk which seems to him the problem, but who his employer is. The accountants imagine that if only their boss were stronger, they would like their jobs better, although many of them fled from exactly such a person in the past. Miss Bowen felt that the people who ought to have been authorities were never strong enough. This negative imagination is wholly under the aegis of the existing order. It disbelieves, but only to dream of someone else, not of a different way of life.

# II

# Recognition

# 4

# The Unhappy Consciousness

## HEGEL'S JOURNEY

In 1807, at the age of thirty-seven, Hegel published his first major work, *The Phenomenology of the Spirit*. The book was completed in an atmosphere of turmoil, for the previous year Napoleon had seized the city of Jena, where Hegel had been teaching; Hegel fled his lodgings with half the manuscript and little else. The *Phenomenology* shows the philosopher taking a rather different view toward society than did the young Hegel in his impassioned reaction to the events of the French Revolution. Negation, so important in his earlier attitudes, as in the writings of Fichte and Schlegel, is still there. But now this idea has been expanded, enriched, and set alongside another term: recognition.

In perhaps the most famous chapter of the *Phenomenology*, "Lordship and Bondage," Hegel gives a succinct definition of this term. At the outset of the chapter, he writes that a whole human being exists "only in being acknowledged." This entails a "process of [mutual] recognition." Simply to shut out another person's existence, whether it is good or evil, powerful or weak, would mean one is an incomplete person oneself. The idea of recognition might seem trivial; as the cliché has it, no man is an island. But this idea has too a tragic meaning in the psychology of authority.

Authority is, we have seen, a matter of defining and interpreting differences in strength. In one sense, the sentiment of authority is the recognition just that these differences exist. In another sense, a more complicated one, it is a matter of taking account of the needs and desires of the weak as well as of the strong once these differences have been acknowledged.

Louis Dumont's study of Indian civilization in *Homo Hierarchicus* and Le Roy Ladurie's picture of medieval Provence in *Montaillou* are portraits of lives locked into hierarchies of strength; at each level people look for someone above to do, think, or interpret what they cannot accomplish themselves. No shame attached to this dependence, so natural a structure of living with other people did it seem. It is curious to the modern reader, because he or she is modern, to hear the bishops and peasants of medieval Provence speak to each other with respect, as unequals.

One could regret the loss of these societies, by romanticizing poverty, superstition, and legal slavery. Yet the very fact of their existence is suggestive: psychological recognition and social difference were combined. To the modern intelligence, these are dissonant elements. What medievalism suggested to Hegel was the relation of recognition and difference as a wholly psychological phenomenon. He attempted to create a picture of a long inner journey in search of fulfilling authority in which these elements play back and forth with each other; at the end of the journey would be not a happy society of kings and castes but a stressful, divided consciousness in which a person feels the force of authority and yet is free. For all Hegel's special philosophic concerns and convoluted language, the nature of the journey he describes suggests, I believe, how the experience of authority might become less humiliating, more free in everyday life.

Hegel asks us first to imagine something like a duel. Two people battle each other for attention. Notice me; I am noticing you only because I want you to take account of what I want. Hegel says, "They must engage in this struggle, for they must raise their certainty of being for themselves to truth"; that is, if you take account of my needs and desires in the way you act, then they are real and I am real. But this battle to elicit recognition from someone else is not a duel to the death. If I vanquished your spirit so totally that you became an abject slave, a nonentity, I would have won a Pyrrhic victory. No one different from me would be acknowledging my existence. I need instead an Other, some distinct person to make those signs of appreciation, deference, and obedience which tell me that what I want matters. This victory which stops short of death, this unequal establishing of whose needs and desires matter, is the relationship Hegel calls that between lordship and bondage.

Jessica Benjamin suggests this relationship is best thought of in terms of the pleasure which power gives. Hegel, she says, believes that the powerful person can take pleasure by virtue of his power; the person in bondage furnishes the means for this pleasure—not only by the pure psychological processes of flattery and attention, but also by working for the lord. The bondsman creates things which the lord uses for enjoyment and, like Nero gesturing toward the Roman fleet and saying "All that is for me," gives the lord a sense of his own worth. There is an irony in this work, however, an irony which ultimately will set the bondsman free.

The lord is dependent on the bondsman for producing his pleasure. True, he may be able to starve his vassal, beat him, abuse him—but this sheer dominance gives him only sadistic pleasure in return. By employing the threat of these punishments instead, the lord hopes to induce his bondsman to produce more, psychologically and materially. But what the bondsman makes is outside the relationship between himself and his lord. He may make a fur robe for the lord's pleasure. Its production involves standards of craftsmanship independent of the lord's pleasure in the object itself. "The lord," Hegel says, "relates himself mediately to the bondsman through a thing that is independent . . . the lord is the power over this thing . . ." but the robe and the master are not one.

The irony, then, begins in the fact that the lord needs a bondsman in order to experience pleasure and confirm himself: "The truth of the independent consciousness is accordingly the servile consciousness of the bondsman." The irony culminates in the fact that the work the bondsman does for his master ultimately takes him outside the terms of pure dominance and obedience. "Through work," Hegel says, "the bondsman becomes conscious of what he truly is." The first step outside bondage is the inferior's discovery, through thinking about his work in relation to himself, "that he has a mind of his own." At that moment, he has begun to cut free.

The young Hegel thought that the burden of establishing conditions of liberty in society lay with the oppressed; no benevolent Platonic guardian, no necessary angel, would come to the rescue. The Hegel of the *Phenomenology* has clarified this idea. Hegel does so by defining the birth of liberty—in the bondsman's consciousness of his work. He then describes the stages of liberty through which the bondsman passes. There are four of these stages, and the movement from each to the next occurs when the oppressed negates what he or she had formerly believed.

These four stages are stoicism, scepticism, the unhappy consciousness, and rational consciousness. They begin with the stoic's withdrawal from the world into his or her own thought, a primitive, inward freedom. The scepticism of the next stage turns toward the world: the bondsman, still an obedient servant, nonetheless disbelieves in the role he acts and in the lord's moral superiority. The unhappy consciousness takes this sceptical knowledge about a social relationship inside; there is a lord and a bondsman in every human being. Hegel calls unhappy consciousness "consciousness of self as a dual-natured, *merely* contradictory being." In a rational consciousness this knowledge again becomes social; the unhappy schism each person feels in himself he also sees in others. Hegel calls this final stage of freedom "rational" because now the person can perceive and act with others according to common purposes; there is no longer the need to fight others for recognition, since one's own consciousness is so developed that one knows the divisions within oneself are divisions that exist in all humanity. Hegel also calls this rational, purposive consciousness an "absolute" state of freedom, and the use of the word "absolute" is a key to his overall intentions: "Of the absolute it must be said that it is essentially a result, that only in the end is it what it truly is."

This is the journey. The stations of the journey are marked by crises of authority. Crises of authority are constructed around the modulations in recognizing freedom and slavery in oneself, recognizing them in other human beings, and recognizing oneself in other human beings. Each crisis occurs through disbelieving what one previously believed. But these acts of disbelieving are not ends. They are means to new patterns of belief. During the later phases of this churning over, when one recognizes with distress the lord and servant within oneself, and then the lord and servant within others, the upheavals alter the way one acts with other human beings. In the latter two phases, the old lord loses his power over the bondsman, not because the bondsman overthrows him or takes his place but because the unhappy bondsman becomes a different human being, one who deals with the lord non-competitively; this forces the lord to modulate his own behavior.

The idea that authority is renewed by periodic crises is perhaps the most radical element of Hegel's theory. Consciousness of lordship and bondage is all: crises change the nature of a person's consciousness. More and more the ethics of recognition—sympathy, sensitivity, modesty about oneself—should control the interpretation of power. This free recognition *is* freedom.

It is an enormously idealistic, spiritual view, but anything but a naïve concept of liberty. Liberty is not happiness. It is experience of division, it is the final acknowledgement that a tyrant and a slave live in every human being; only by acknowledging this fact can human beings ever hope to be more than duelists. Liberty finally exists when the recognition I give you does not subtract something from myself.

If we ask how much this philosophic system describes the concrete realities of our lives, we would first have to say that industrial society since Hegel's time has gone halfway on this journey. The first two Hegelian moments, of stoicism and scepticism, are everyday experiences, but they have not ripened into the later stages of freedom Hegel envisioned. Disobedient dependence, for instance, may be thought of as a perverse form of Hegelian scepticism. I rebel against you, I violate you, I say you are unworthy, and therefore I make myself feel safe in your hands. I become obsessed with what you would think or do in order to sneer and do the opposite —and so the knot of your control over my life tightens even though I am disobedient. The fantasy of disappearance is a sort of infantile scepticism: I imagine that if I disbelieve in you, you will cease to hold me. Idealized substitution is the most complicated: I imagine personal authority to be like the production of a photograph. Whatever you are in the flesh is the negative; the positive is the ideal; that is the opposite of you. But it is your image I am always printing. None of these negations move further toward the redefinition of social relationships Hegel envisioned in the latter two stages of his journey.

The reason these ways of disbelief in personal authority close in upon themselves has ultimately to do with the kinds of authority which are subject to attack. We most easily imagine omnipotent authority in terms of tyrannies like Nazism. Hegel understood that authority also could be omnipotent, in the sense of absolute, as long as it was conceived to be external. I think the problem is out there, the oppressors are external, I'm just serving my time and I don't believe in them or what I'm doing. If I don't recognize myself as a participant in this oppression, then the oppressors are unchecked. I disbelieve, and they rule. The dominant forms of personal authority in modern industrial society have the capacity to provoke enormous amounts of such disaffection. There are two poles of this dominant authority. One is an authority without love, the authority of personal autonomy. It operates by principles of indifference to others and self-sufficing expertise which absorbs rebellion from below yet exerts powerful controls of shame on those who are rebellious. The other used to be characteristic of individual capitalists, and now appears in bureaucracies, socialist and capitalist alike. It is an authority of false love, the authority of paternalism. It operates as a parade of benevolence which exists only so far as it is in the interest of the ruler and which requires passive acquiescence as the price of being cared for.

Around either of these poles, disobedient dependence, fantasies of disappearance, and idealized substitution revolve, as with the aborigines in New Guinea who regularly, ritually, threaten their chief; having insulted him, denied him, discharged their anger toward him, they remain his subjects.

If we ask how the journey Hegel imagines may be continued, we have to consider three issues. First: how exactly does a crisis of authority occur so that a person does not fall back to where he or she was before? Hegel asserts that this happens, but does not explain in any way the process by which the interpretation of power shifts. This issue is especially important given the stage of the journey we have not yet taken —the stage of unhappy consciousness in which the oppositional, us-against-them mentality is overcome and a person comes to conceive of the origins of servitude as a conundrum of inner desire. How does such a massive shift in consciousness occur? We then have immediately to face a second issue. In what sort of world would this unhappiness make sense? I don't mean abstractly, but in terms of how people deal with their bosses, with their children rebelling against school, with the tentacles of the government which touch ordinary life. The unhappy consciousness prompts people to believe in authority without believing in the omnipotence of a person in authority; neither the enemy nor salvation is outside the gates, both are desires within consciousness; to seek them as pure essences of other people is to lie to oneself. No one can heal this inner division—and yet such a thing as authority exists. What is the shape of power in ordinary society consonant with this knowledge? What does power without omnipotence look like?

These two issues lead to a destination different from Hegel's. He arrived at the vision of a cooperative, rational society. The processes by which a crisis of authority brings into being an unhappy consciousness, and the society which supports this consciousness, force us to think of authority in much darker terms. The Greeks knew this other destination. The Theban plays of Sophocles are all about acts of recognition which dethrone ultimate authority; the plays are tragedies. Alongside the Athenian love of rational order is a distrust of the human capacity to order the world. This distrust, this fear of *hubris,* was thought to set a person free. A free person believed there are rules but no Rule. And, unlike the happy nostrums of modern liberalism founded on a somewhat similar idea, the Athenians knew that rules without Rule are unfulfilling, like a hunger which remains unsatisfied in the name of health. To think, then, of the evolution of authority so that it is more free, more liberal in the true sense, poses a moral question at the roots of Western civilization. How much exposure to uncertainty, to half measures, to unhappiness can humanity bear in order to be free?

The present chapter is about how a crisis of authority may lead a person to renounce visions of a satisfying, omnipotent authority. The next chapter is about the conditions of power in everyday life which would be consonant with that renunciation. The final chapter of the essay concerns the moral question posed by this journey.

A crisis of authority which leads to renouncing an authority as omnipotent has a definite structure. First there is detachment from the influence of the authority. Then there follows a reflexive question: what was I like under that authority's influence? Once the work of detachment and reflection is done, a question can be asked about the person in authority: is his or her influence legitimate? Only when this question comes at the end can it be asked freely, with neither the compulsion to give a negative answer nor the desire to satisfy a hidden agenda. This sequence is something of an irony, for only when we have learned to remove ourselves from the sphere of authority can we re-enter it, with a sense of its limits and a knowledge of how commands and obedience might be changed so that our real needs for protection and reassurance might be served.

This sequence has no rigid timetable. Months can pass between the moment a woman leaves her marriage and the moment she feels strong enough to face what she was really like under her husband's sway, months filled with formulaic explanations which suddenly appear stale. Or the sequence can unfold rapidly, as with a son who, hard on the heels of realizing that he was not simply his father's victim, perceives that his father was more than a victimizer. Any sequence which gives consciousness a structure is, as William James remarked, a "catalyst": thinking about $x$ permits me to think more openly about $y$. In technical terms, there is a necessary "evolutionary ontology" in performing interpretive tasks. In this case, to think about the legitimacy of an authority figure without having first disengaged from that figure and explored oneself is likely to mean one would think nothing very new; the unexplored, inner voices of one's own needs and injuries would remain in control.

Equally, the sequence of interpretation must be fulfilled for the experience of authority to be understood. Simply to become detached, or to remain self-absorbed, would not be enough to make sense of what is essentially a relationship *between* people. There is a structure to experiences of crisis, then, just as there is a structure to periods of relative stability, and this structure resides in stages by which a certain destination is reached, rather than by a rigid timetable for the journey.

## DISENGAGEMENT

The first step any person must take to reconceive authority is to disengage from it temporarily. This first step is the most perilous. Often what seem to be the most radical breaks turn out to be illusory. A striking instance of this illusion appears in the writing and life of the French Jacobin Saint-Just. In his *Institutions* he proclaims:

> Everything that exists around us must change and come to an end, because everything around us is unjust . . . obliged to isolate himself from the world and from himself, man drops his anchor in the future and presses to his heart the posterity which bears no blame for the evils of the present. . . .

This break with the past is based on a pathological pride. Of himself as a free revolutionary, Saint-Just says:

> I have left all weakness behind me; I have seen only the truth in the universe and I have expressed it.

Immense political consequences flowed from this pathology. There was in fact no greater liberty under the regime Saint-Just helped inaugurate; a new slavery arose to take the place of the old. "Liberty," Saint-Just proclaimed at the height of the Terror,

> must prevail at any price. . . . You must not merely punish traitors but the indifferent as well; you must punish whoever is passive in the republic. . . . We must rule by iron those who cannot be ruled by justice.

The pathology of Saint-Just is an extreme instance of illusory disengagement. Disbelieving in one set of reasons for power —the authority of the *ancien régime*—has not lead to distrust of power itself, and certainly not to distrust of his own power. It was in making sense of such figures that Hegel came to the conclusion that the first step in becoming free was not simply the overthrow of existing power, but a moment of detachment from the world of power altogether. Then power can be truly perceived, both inside and outside oneself.

How is the first stage of detachment to come into being? There are two distinct paths along which it can be created. One is through the creation of a mask. The other is through a purge.

A mask which allows one to disengage is vividly described by Edmund Gosse in his autobiography, *Father and Son.* One day the young Gosse finds his father to be in error about a fact he stoutly maintained to be true. "My father," Gosse writes,

> . . . as a deity, as a natural force of immense prestige, fell in my eyes to a human level. In future, his statements about things in general need not be accepted implicitly.

The discovery of his father's fallibility did not make the young man rebellious, nor did he directly call his father to account. Instead, a part of him withdrew from his father. Gosse says that

> . . . of all the thoughts which rushed upon my savage and undeveloped little brain at this crisis, the most curious was that I had found a companion and a confidant in myself. There was a secret in this world and it belonged to me and to a somebody who lived in the same body with me.

The German term for this consciousness is exact: the *Doppelgänger* (roughly, an alternate sense of self, a double being). "There were two of us," Gosse writes, "and we could talk with one another. . . ."

> It is difficult to define impressions so rudimentary, but is certain that it was in this dual form that the sense of my individuality now suddenly descended upon me, and it is equally certain that it was a great solace to me to find a sympathiser in my own breast.

The story then told in Gosse's autobiography is how one little boy watches the other obey, watches how meekness and silence mark the features of the obedient child, observes the father interpret these signs of obedience as if they were his boy's true character. Finally, when the young man is in his middle teens, the features of the obedient child have become so false-seeming that the young man in an angry moment removes the mask. Another person stands revealed to his father, not so much rebellious or combative as alien. The sense of wearing a mask is more than a protective matter. It permitted the child over a period of five years to evaluate his father's authority and his own responses.

Images of a masked self have a long history. They were in the Renaissance a way to explain how perfectly normal-seeming women could also be witches. In Dostoevsky's *The Double*, the Renaissance imagery is reversed, the "normal" person being worldly and wicked, and the secret person tormenting him a man of decency. Serious psychological exploration of the image of a double self has not focused so much on Jekylls and Hydes (this popular stereotype of literally two unrelated personalities sharing the same body being extremely rare in fact) as it has on the purposes which are served by a belief that there are alternative organizations one can make of one's consciousness. Phyllis Greenacre has studied, for instance, the relation of a sense of double self to artistic creativity, the secret self playing with sensations which the surface self has classified into routine categories and so become numb to. In psychopathological work, the Renaissance image of being haunted has reappeared in the idea that a *Doppelgänger* is a paranoid fantasy; all the dangerous, repressed feelings of a person are organized as a secret self which torments the normal person who has found his or her place in "reality."

The image born in the Renaissance of being tormented by a second self may obscure the fact that the *Doppelgänger* phenomenon is also a way to work on reality itself, and particularly to work on making sense of patterns of power. What it provides in the life of a young man like Gosse is, first of all, a shelter from someone else's commands; part of the young man cannot be touched. Second, it removes commands from the status of being moral absolutes; if part of the young man cannot be touched, then the commands are not omnipotent. Third, the whole power relation can be observed: how one responds, as well as what one is told to do.

A mask offers these strengths of detachment. But it is also subject to dangers. The conviction that there is a hidden person the master can't touch may become simply a conviction without a definition, as in this instance of a twenty-six-year-old man who married a woman against his mother's wishes:

*Interviewer:*   When did you tell your mother you were going to get married?

*Subject:*   About two weeks before we actually did.

*Interviewer:*   You said you were going to level with her, show her what you really felt . . . how exactly?

*Subject:*   I thought that once we really got down to it in this thing, she'd see me the way I really am. Funny, but after the explosion, there was nothing I wanted to say to her, I mean . . . it surprised me. I thought I'd act real different toward her, but I didn't have that much different feeling than I had before. I just thought I had something much different inside.

The separation between an outer, obedient figure and an inner observer can also lead to passivity of a kind we are already familiar with. The outer self goes through the motions. The inner self disbelieves all that the outer self performs—this "real" self becomes a source of negation, but also a permanent region of indifference. Since it isn't really "me" obeying and cooperating with my parents, I can go along; my actions don't really matter, since I don't really believe in them.

This mask serves positive ends only if the division between outer and observing self is uncertain and jarring, if the two modes do not make peace with each other. The environment of which the person is conscious plays an important role in making this masking temporary or not; parents distant from and unconcerned about what their children feel invite the children to hide for good behind a docile mask, as does an indifferent boss. An intrusive parent like Gosse's father may force the issue. But the character of the mask, a consciousness of what it is, also plays a role. A person must conceive of his or her mask of obedience as serving a purpose. The mask is an instrument: it gives an opportunity to observe with safety. It should not be a sanctuary or an end in itself.

A mask is a way of sheltering someone from influence or seduction by an authority. The logically opposite path of disengagement is to purge the influences. Purge rituals are familiar in anthropology: the exorcism which wards off evil spirits, the rite of passage in which the adolescent erases childish fears through an exploit or a test. As Mary Douglas has pointed out in *Purity and Danger,* a purge is an act people perform because they fear that the danger is inside, that they have been seduced and have yielded. Pure coercive power would be a one-way influence; the purge is aimed at dealing with the fact that the person is responding. The attempt to disengage through purging oneself is a universal phenomenon; it appears in the most complicated circumstances as well as the simplest. Here is a complicated and notorious example.

In the wake of a trip André Gide made to England in the company of a seventeen-year-old boy, Gide's wife, Madeleine, burned all his letters to her, something like two thousand letters covering his youth and middle age. "All the best of me I had entrusted to those letters," Gide wrote in his *Journal Intime;*

> . . . they were not exactly love-letters; effusiveness disgusts me, and she would never have endured being praised . . . but in them the pattern of my life was woven before her eyes, little by little and day by day.

Three days after she told Gide that she had burned the record of his life, Madeleine Gide also told him:

After you left, when I found myself all alone again in the big house that you were abandoning, without a single person on whom I could lean, no longer knowing what to do, what would become of me . . . I burned your letters in order to have something to do. Before I destroyed them I read them all over, one by one. . . . They were the most precious thing I owned in the world.

The statement that she destroyed what was most precious to her captures the essence of a purge. Neither in anthropological nor psychological lore does it appear as a parallel to the physical purges of modern medicine. Not the relief of pain, but the infliction of sustained pain upon oneself is the act, in order that something destructive even if pleasurable to the human being may be expelled. In rites of passage in New Guinea, the tests of valor an adolescent performs are to teach him that he will not survive if he continues to enjoy the soft pleasures he knew as a child. For Madeleine Gide, protecting and caring for André Gide had been a role and a source of maternal pleasure since her childhood; burning Gide's correspondence was an apt way of pushing this pleasure out of her life. Gide claimed to have written her constantly whenever they were apart, and they had known each other since childhood.

On the eve of Gide's trip to England in 1918 with his young boy, Madeleine Gide wrote her husband the following letter. (The dating of this letter was finally established by Jean Schlumberger; I have set in italics one sentence.)

André Dear,
    You are mistaken. I have no doubts of your affection. And even if I had, I should have nothing to complain of. My portion has been a handsome one: I have had the best of your soul, the tenderness of your childhood and your youth. . . . I have always understood, moreover, your need to move from place to place, your need for freedom. How many times in your fits of nervous anguish —the price you pay for your genius—have these words been on the tip of my tongue: *"But my dear, leave, go, you are free, there is no door on the cage, nothing is keeping you here. . . ."* What pains me—and you know it without my saying so—is the road

down which you are traveling and which is going to lead you and others to perdition. Again please believe that I am not saying this with any feeling of condemnation. I pity you as much as I love you. . . .

This particular affair, however, turned out to be a breaking point, in part because the young man involved was not a newcomer to the Gides' adult life, but a boy whose family was intimately involved with their own past. Marc Allègret was the son of the Protestant missionary Elie Allègret. Elie Allègret, in the words of David Littlejohn, "helped prepare young André for his first Communion in 1886; stood as his best man in 1895; and later entrusted his sons, and especially Marc, to Gide's tutorial care." Under these conditions Madeleine Gide, a devout Protestant, reached a breaking point in her toleration of Gide's affairs. As Gide's trip was drawing to its conclusion, she began the process of reading and destroying his letters.

The consequences of this act were not to destroy their marriage, or even its outer appearance of stability. Rather, the legitimacy of Gide's demands for comfort and support was broken in her mind. He was no longer The Artist to whom all things were allowed in the name of his genius. The dual existence which André Gide had previously led, it should be said, was no idyll for him; this sexless marriage made him feel he was rotting, and even as he sought his wife's comforts, and her presence as a refuge, he felt himself living a lie. For Madeleine Gide, the rupture was also clarifying; it "broke the spell," as she later remarked. She withdrew from concern about Gide's creative struggles, never reading another of his books, devoting herself to the life of the countryside and to religious matters which had interested her since her youth.

The structure of this purge may seem its most bizarre aspect, Madeleine Gide rereading each letter she was to burn. But it is the structure of this ritual act which connects it to other, more mundane experiences of the same sort. Something is made known, present to consciousness, felt once again, and then destroyed. The other person isn't destroyed; Madeleine Gide has no thought to leave or humiliate her husband. Only the fetishes of her involvement are broken.

This structure resembles an element of the mask; its purpose too is to serve as a means of breaking involvement, rather than declaring war. Both the mask and the purge are heuristic devices in a crisis of authority; that is, instruments of self-teaching. The psychoanalyst Ernest Schachtel has sought to characterize the universality of such devices by saying they are instruments for the "emergence from embeddedness." By this phrase Schachtel means that a person has to teach himself or herself that what exists is not given forever; nothing is embedded permanently. Schachtel's concern is the human body *per se.* The body grows and decays, yet at any given moment people act as though their organic state is fixed: they *are* children or they *are* adults. The sense of being a creature in a continual state of metamorphosis is, in Schachtel's view, a difficult human insight; psychologically we are more secure if we imagine our present condition to be the essence of ourselves. For this reason any instrument which removes us from a sense of embeddedness is a device which causes us pain, throws us into the anxieties of flux, and not incidentally forces us to confront biological fact.

This psychoanalytic insight has a bearing on the domain of authority. Valéry expressed it one way by saying that every ruler knows how fragile the authority of rulers is—except for his own. The concept of embeddedness has a rather different meaning to his subjects. They may indeed remain servants all their lives, to an ever-changing set of masters. To disrupt their servitude, they must disrupt a sense of the naturalness of being a servant. That disruption requires a delicate operation, either a painful purge of old attachments or a shelter from the master's influence, so that both sides—rule and service—may be witnessed and weighed in the balance.

This delicate operation of detachment is how all crises of authority begin. What distinguishes the detachment of the young Gosse or Madeleine Gide from the negations of Miss Bowen or the apocalyptic mentality of a Saint-Just is that the first step is a recognition of the sheer seriousness of authority. Whatever impression another person's authority made, the impression was deep and cannot be effaced by a single liberating act of will.

## THE VICTIM

Once recognition of the seriousness of authority occurs, the most important issue a person must face is how exactly the authority made him or her act. The mind's vision of this influence is often depressing: mortifying things done to win approval or to attract the authority's notice, injuries of which some were inflicted by the master and some were self-inflicted. It is a landscape in which the subject looms large as a victim.

Often this first image of oneself as a victim is the image which remains in place. Parents or bosses or lovers come into focus as figures who hurt; worse, who cause us to hurt ourselves. Socially, this image was accurately if brutally conveyed by Marx in the idea of a *Lumpenproletariat:* in the shelter of their pubs, the oppressed speak of the burden of their sufferings, feel it as an evil fate, and give up. Nothing can be done; inducing resignation to "fate" is the masters' ultimate weapon. The remarkable stories of V. S. Naipaul's *In a Free State* depict the spirit of a *Lumpenproletariat* spread over an entire society, rich as well as poor. But although most self-conscious victims are telling a true story, they are not telling enough of it. People can also work on this image so that it is in time recomposed. The person can eventually appear to himself or herself as more than someone else's victim. The gain is that authority figures, while still seen as people who may have done harm, are no longer seen as omnipotent in their capacity to inflict pain.

Recomposing this landscape occurs, when it does, through the experience of a simple psychological mechanism of recognition. In the dreams of young parents, the following scene appears occasionally. The parent imagines itself both as a baby and as an adult; a mother may imagine herself in a crib, but, unlike her baby, she is full-sized and her limbs protrude through the bars of the crib while her trunk fills the entire space within. Or a father imagines himself dressed in tiny clothes, shoes which pinch his feet and sweaters which choke his throat. In more familiar waking experiences which parallel such dreams, the young parent, seeing for the first few times its child stumble and cry out, imagines the infant to be in much greater distress than it is; the parent imagines the fall in terms of an adult hitting its head.

These juxtapositions are instances of a process I shall call "doubling." It is identifying with someone else by half, imagining what that person experiences but still keeping the attributes of one's own body, age, and strength. Doubling entails empathy rather than sympathy. This distinction, as put forward by Richard Wollheim, is the difference between saying "I know what it feels like" and "I feel for you." Empathy requires some enquiry into another life, sympathy is more discreet, an expression of concern without an attempt necessarily to understand. Empathic imagination also differs from the creation of a *Doppelgänger,* two versions of oneself; rather, it is oneself imagined in the body or circumstances of another.

The doubling dreams of parents are empathic acts on the part of people who have recently acquired power over the life of other human beings. The doubling serves the purpose of understanding what the controls the parent can exercise will mean to the child: what is it like to be confined to a crib-cage, to be dressed by someone else, to cry instead of speak when one needs something? Doubling is one initiation through fantasy into a new context of power.

This process of recognizing what another person feels can reappear when a scheme of authority established among adults is challenged. It appears in particular as a way of imagining what someone whom one formerly considered authoritative might be like now that one has stripped away the veils of assurance and strength in which he or she was previously shrouded. What sort of influence did the authority exert?

Perhaps the richest documentation of this use of doubling appears in a letter Franz Kafka wrote his father in November of 1919, a letter in which Kafka sets down the issues in their lifelong struggle with each other. The manuscript is in two parts. There are in the first part forty-five typewritten pages. Here Kafka directly addresses his father, explaining from his point of view why their relations have been so miserable. Then Kafka makes the matter doubled. There are two-and-a-half handwritten pages he added in which he imagines what his father's response would be. Finally there is a last, handwritten paragraph which is Kafka's answer to this imagined response. After completing the whole letter, Kafka gave it to his mother to give to his father; she refused to do so, and returned it to Kafka. (Whether or not she read it is unknown.)

The typewritten body of the letter is a powerful and subtle piece of manipulation. Herr Kafka was the wrong kind of father for his son: Franz Kafka was bound to be the wrong kind of son for his father. As a result, Franz Kafka has become a victim, tortured equally by the harshness of his father and by the sense of his own inadequacies. In the handwritten end of the letter, Kafka tries to imagine what comment the elder Kafka would make about his son as a victim. In the body of the letter, authority is perceived in terms of idealized substitution; the opposite of you and me is what we each needed. In the end of the letter, idealized substitution is transcended.

The most graphic example Kafka gives of being victimized by his father is the following childhood punishment. (The *pavlatche* referred to in this incident is a balcony built at the second story around the inner courtyard of traditional Eastern European houses.)

There is only one episode in the early years of which I have a direct memory. You may remember it, too. One night I kept on whimpering for water, not, I am certain, because I was thirsty, but probably partly to be annoying, partly to amuse myself. After several vigorous threats had failed to have any effect, you took me out of bed, carried me out onto the *pavlatche,* and left me there alone for a while in my nightshirt, outside the shut door. I am not going to say that this was wrong—perhaps there was really no other way of getting peace and quiet that night—but I mention it as typical of your methods of bringing up a child and their effect on me. I dare say I was quite obedient afterwards at that period, but it did me inner harm. What was for me a matter of course, that senseless asking for water, and the extraordinary terror of being carried outside were two things that I, my nature being what it was, could never properly connect with each other. Even years afterwards I suffered from the tormenting fancy that the huge man, my father, the ultimate authority, would come almost for no reason at all and take me out of bed in the night and carry me out onto the *pavlatche,* and that meant I was a mere nothing for him.

This memory has the following structure. First there is Kafka's description of himself "whimpering for water," a ruse to gain his parents' attention. Kafka paints himself in malicious colors for what is after all the most ordinary of children's ploys for attention. Then there is the response—a catastrophic over-reaction. His father puts him outside on the balcony, the boy clad only in his nightshirt (at the time these nightshirts were of thin India cotton), and shuts the door. Kafka drives home the knife by the remark which immediately follows this description of the event: "I am not going to say this was wrong ... but I mention it as typical of your methods of bringing up a child and their effect on me." Here is forgiveness, which puts Kafka in a superior position to his father, and then the observation that it is "typical of your methods of bringing up a child." Simply to explain this "example" to his father is the reason Kafka says he wants to "mention" this little incident.

Kafka, now having established his superiority through his charitable understanding, is ready to say how his father was monstrous and himself an innocent victim. "That senseless asking for water" and the "extraordinary terror" of being locked out in the cold, Kafka, as a child, could not understand to be connected. He seems to make this out as something wrong with himself—"my nature being what it was"—but then, what child could connect these things? How unfair of a father to think this was good discipline. And to drive home the horrendousness of his father's action to him, Kafka tells him how much this incident injured him: he suffered for "years afterward." The suffering has two elements. First his father, the "ultimate authority," would come in the night and hurt him "for no reason at all." A complicated statement, surely, since the beginning of the memory is Kafka's assertion of his malicious naughtiness. But then, that confession is not real. I was bad on the surface; underneath, you were truly cruel. The second part of this long-standing injury is that his father's action "meant I was a mere nothing for him." A harsh punishment is equivalent to his father having no love for him.

You couldn't help it, but you made me suffer so. This is how the victim exhibits his wounds in order to fight back against his tormentor. Whatever you say to me, I forgive you—only I suffered so much. Moreover, I am so weak.

In the handwritten passage, Kafka proceeds to test this posture. Despite appearances, Kafka has his father say, "You do not make things more difficult for yourself, but much more profitable." The term "profitable" *(einträglich)* is a nice one. One of Kafka's images of his father is of the man who clawed his way from poverty to middle-class life, retaining all the grossness of a peddler, obsessing continually about money. In the domain of fine feelings, perhaps his son also knows how to turn a smart profit. Kafka's imagined father then spells this out. "You want to be 'overly clever' and 'overly affectionate' at the same time and acquit me also of all guilt." This is a deception, for

> what appears between the lines, in spite of all the fine phrases about character and nature and antagonism and helplessness, is that actually I have been the aggressor, while everything you did was self-defense.

Kafka's imagined father then is able to call his son's own game of power to account. The son pretends out of sheer magnanimity you are ready not only to forgive me but (what is both more and less) also to prove and be willing to believe yourself that—contrary to the truth—I am also not guilty.

Kafka's imagined father will have none of this false sweetness —a sweet smile to hide the pain, a smile whose real purpose is to overwhelm Father with guilt.

This play between what Kafka says to his father and the imagined response of his father is one way the psychological process of doubling can transcend a specific kind of immobilizing negation. Idealized substitution is called to account because it is exposed as a weapon in the young Kafka's attempt to make the elder Kafka feel guilty: neither of us is what the other needed. In this substitution the young Kafka gets to be the victim; this, too, the doubling also calls into account. It is important to note that this change is internal, a Hegelian moment of recognition. The bondsman has taken it upon himself to stage a battle which has failed to occur in real life, and to learn from that battle in his head.

This imaginative work on power is far different from the famous despairing statement of Rousseau, in the *Nouvelle Héloïse,* of how he sought in fantasy to escape from a recalcitrant world of fact:

The impossibility of grasping realities threw me into the land of chimeras, and seeing nothing in existence that was worthy of my enthusiasm I sought nourishment for it in an ideal world, which my fertile imagination soon peopled with beings after my own heart.

Kafka's imagined father is no "being after his own heart." It is generally true of acts of doubling that they permit hostility to coexist for a time with insight into another person's possible feelings and perceptions. Here the distinction between empathy and sympathy again comes into play. Sympathy presupposes goodwill toward another. Empathy does not. It originates in a desire to see more fully than one has when using fixed images from the past.

What are the consequences of this empathic act? In the letter Kafka writes his father, the most obvious consequence is that Kafka sets himself free from nourishing his own wounds. But there is something more. The last paragraph of the whole manuscript is Kafka's attempt to work out the sense of what his imagined father has said. It is as follows:

> My answer to this is that, after all, this whole rejoinder—which can partly also be turned against you—does not come from you, but from me. Not even your mistrust of others is as great as my self-mistrust, which you have bred in me. I do not deny a certain justification for this rejoinder, which in itself contributes new material to the characterization of our relationship. Naturally things cannot in reality fit together the way the evidence does in my letter; life is more than a Chinese puzzle. But with the correction made by this rejoinder—a correction I neither can nor will elaborate in detail—in my opinion something has been achieved which so closely approximates the truth that it might reassure us both a little and make our living and our dying easier.
>
> Franz

The first third of this paragraph echoes Kafka's game again: "Not even your mistrust of others [i.e., me] is as great as my self-mistrust, which you have bred in me." I am wounded; it's your fault. Then the view modulates, not to one of forgiveness but to distance, objectivity. The imagined father "contributes new material" to the actual relation between father and son. Then Kafka makes a statement innocent of guilt or pride—"in my opinion something has been achieved which so closely approximates the truth that it might reassure us both a little. . . ." The work of the letter is complete: antagonists and manipulators of each other as father and son remain, thanks to this letter they now have a picture of their life, something outside the circle of recrimination.

This bears on Hegel's idea that there is no freedom until the end, until all the stages of negation have been worked through. In Kafka's letter there are the initial arias of injury, accusation, and forgiveness, the doubled reply, the response in turn to a father whose straight talk has to be imagined. At the conclusion of this process, Kafka steps back and speaks with assurance about understanding the relationship. This voice is far stronger than the voice which appears at the opening of the letter, a voice whose only power lies in its capacity to arouse guilt.

The moral status of the victim has never been greater or more dangerous than it is now. In Christian theology Christ was man's victim, but He was not ennobled by His suffering. He is a god, not a hero. In Piero della Francesca's *Flagellation* in Urbino, we are presented, for example, with His flagellation in the left half of the picture and a group of Renaissance gentlemen in the right totally unconcerned by His suffering. Just as He is not ennobled, they are not humanly demeaned by their indifference; they are fallen spiritually. Similarly, the poor of this world are not heroes; they suffer and they will be redeemed. Their oppressors are not monsters, only human. As this Christian notion of the non-heroic victim began to wane in the Enlightenment, a new image of those who suffered was born. The capacity to suffer is a sign of human courage; the masses are heroic; their suffering is the best measure of social injustice. Those who oppress them are not to be pitied, a pity due finally to all humanity in its fall from grace; the secular oppressors are simply an enemy to be destroyed.

The ennobling of suffering was the moral foundation of Romanticism: the artist who suffered in the midst of a vulgar horde, the poor who suffered at the hands of the callous. In politics this elevation of the victim invited a particular group of abuses. Sympathy was extended to the victim for his condition, not as a person; if he improved his material circumstances or was mobile upward socially, then he lost his moral claims; he was "a traitor to his class." If he suffered at the hands of society but was content with his lot, then he lacked true consciousness about himself. Much more pervasive than these special cases was the notion which flowered in the Romantic era and continues strong today that no person is morally legitimate unless he or she is suffering. The sources of legitimacy through suffering are ultimately to be found in an injury inflicted by someone else or by "the environment." In contemporary life this idea of moral legitimacy finds a voice, for instance, in the recent writings of R. D. Laing. In Laing's view, the schizophrenic knows, by virtue of suffering, truths about the psyche which no one else knows; the causes of the suffering are a schizophrenogenic society. The idea finds another voice in the recent Maoist writings of Jean-Paul Sartre. Only the worker has claims to "moral hegemony," because only the worker is exposed to the "terrors" of advanced capitalism.

Ennobling the victim devalues ordinary bourgeois life. "Compared to someone in Harlem . . ."—but we are not living in Harlem. Bourgeois morality becomes a morality of the surrogate; the bourgeoisie champions the causes of the oppressed, speaks for those who cannot speak for themselves. This tendency to live off the oppressed for a sense of one's own moral purpose is a devious game. Even if one rejects the life of a Saint-Just, who used the suffering of the unfortunate as a pretext for his own drives for power, one commits something of the same sin by taking the oppressed as "models," as people who are "really" dealing with life, people more solid and substantial than oneself. It is psychological cannibalism. But most of all, the ennobling of victims means that in ordinary middle-class life we are forced constantly to go in search of some injury, some affliction, in order to justify even the contemplation of questions of justice, right, and entitlement in our lives. It is hard to conceive of remaking social relations without contrasting beliefs about what should be against the shadows of injury. The need to legitimate one's beliefs in terms of an injury or suffering to which one has been subjected attaches people more and more to the injuries themselves. In psychotherapeutic work, this legitimation appears continually: "what I need" defined in terms of "what I was denied," so that the act of understanding the denial, the nature of the wound, becomes the entire focus of concern.

The strength to transcend wearing one's injuries as badges of honor is what appears in a document like Kafka's letter to his father. The transcendence is hard-won, culturally as well as personally. The conditions which nourish this strength are extraordinary in cultural terms as well. A crisis of authority is generated by a person who has indubitably suffered at the hands of an authority—his father—and the process of the crisis is conducted in such a way that he gains the strength to admit his need, his attachment. He acquires a strength which seems a paradox. He makes himself vulnerable through an imaginative act of self-criticism. That this letter is so unusual a document is as much a comment on us, his readers, as on the writer.

Hegel speaks of unhappy consciousness as the moment when a person recognizes both slave and master within. No longer "poor little me" oppressed by the world, but somehow also the recognition that the oppressor is inside me. What sort of oppressor finally is it?

In classical political thought, the answer to this question was frequently given in terms of the idea of voluntary servitude. People are too timid, too desirous of routine comfort, too ignorant, to do without masters; they want to be slaves in order to be secure. It is sloth which is the master inside the voluntary servants. Here is the doctrine as expressed by the 16th Century political writer La Boétie:

> ... so many men, so many villages, so many cities, so many nations, sometimes suffer under a single tyrant who has no other power than the power they give him; who could do them absolutely no injury unless they preferred to put up with him rather than contradict him . . . it is therefore the inhabitants themselves who permit, or rather, bring about, their own servitude. A people enslaves itself, cuts its throat . . . gives consent to its own misery, or rather, apparently welcomes it. . . . It is the stupid and cowardly who are neither able to endure hardship nor to vindicate their rights; they stop at merely longing for them, and lose through timidity the valor roused by the effort to claim their rights, although the desire to be free still remains a part of their nature.

Freud's *Beyond the Pleasure Principle* is the culmination of this classic school of thought: to acquire freedom means muffling the voices of pleasure. Unlike the social scientists who believe in the puppetry of socialization, this school accords to humanity an active role in the shaping of its own existence; people actively seek pleasure at the expense of freedom.

Certainly this is a grim idea of freedom, echoing Oscar Wilde's not-so-flippant remark that the trouble with socialism is that it would take too many evenings. But could we say of Miss Bowen, Dr. Dodds, and the Kafka of the first part of the letter that they feel pleasure even as they participate in their own bondage? Miss Bowen attempts to make her dependence on her father safe, but her language is hardly that of a secure, contented person. The regressions of Dr. Dodds to an infantile, needful rage against his employer are filled with pain, not pleasure.

The master within these victims is a rather special master who accords recognition. They have struck a secret treaty with him in their own minds. He will hurt them, and they will be justified, by virtue of their suffering, in demanding his attention, sympathy, regard. The real, external master knows nothing of this secret treaty; he sees his subjects as under his spell, and that is enough. The master they have made is a master who will listen, if only they can justify themselves. And the more they plumb their suffering, the more justified they are.

Dr. Dodds's experience is an extreme example of indifference that everybody has been subjected to in dealing with "the authorities" in state welfare bureaucracies, factories, and offices: they are deaf; they do not accord recognition. The special master, therefore, is a compensatory figure, a wish rooted in experience. Through him pass the voices of condescension, irony, or lack of interest from the outer world; but now, inside, these pains constitute a claim on the master. This inner treaty between master and subject is not an arcane psychological phenomenon. Children assume it exists when they make manipulative use of their crying; adults assume it exists when they guilt-monger. But the manager of a factory who is conveniently deaf is likely to remain so if his employees tell him how much they hurt. He is likely to think in terms of a palliative or immediate remedy—and why not? He could hardly accept the fact that his employees are keeping score of the reasons for a basic change in their mutual relations, a change the employees expect eventually to earn by their pains. And in any event they keep this larger expectation secret. It is their form of compensating themselves, even though it absorbs the victim still more in the slights and unhappinesses which make him deserving.

Kafka's letter is an instance of breaking the terms of this secret treaty by publishing it. And the moral of publication is clear: if people can focus on how they react to being hurt as the real problem, then at the least they will cease to value their injuries; they will not conspire at their own suffering.

The role of the dominant institutions in this conspiracy is complex. On the one hand, in cultural terms, victims have now immense moral prestige. They gain attention of the news media; bureaucrats pay much more attention to people in their care who voice discontent than those who do not. One school of social thought, represented in France by Alain Touraine and in Germany by Jurgen Habermas, argues that the attention paid to society's victims has the paradoxical effect of reinforcing the moral authority of the managers. People turn to the managers to take care of the problems of which those who suffer complain; this "crisis mentality" focuses attention on the managers, the people at the top, as those who can and ought to fix things. On the other hand, institutions and their leaders respond to cries of injury only on the surface: how can we make it hurt less? More money? Shorter hours? This crisis mentality ignores the hidden, unspoken complaint that there is something basically wrong. Suffering is demeaned into a practical problem. If it is material, then it can, literally, be managed. Meanwhile, the servants are secretly keeping score.

The journey Hegel proposes is for them. It is an exit from this manipulable world of material slights and wounds, an invitation to enter into a period of reflection upon what the nature of being wounded means. That meaning ultimately invites the servants to know more about the masters than the masters know about themselves—namely, that the masters are not personally responsible for the harm they do. They are as much prisoners of social conventions and the necessary fictions of domination as those who fall under their sway. The moment the managers are not held personally responsible, at that moment they are not completely in control.

This Hegelian journey is what appealed to Marx; it is what is radical in Hegel's thought, both politically and psychologically. Psychologically this stage of the journey can lead people to empathize with those who they also know have been the instruments of causing them pain. And when that happens, a fundamental power perceived in the person of the authority can be broken: his or her power to inspire fear. As long as one perceives an authority as the source of pain, the authority is indeed potent and fearful. What happens to the image of the person in authority when this bond of fear is then broken? Is an authority inevitably rendered illegitimate?

## LEGITIMACY AND THE FEAR OF AUTHORITY

Personal authority is not based simply on abstract principles of right. As we have seen in the first chapter of this essay, the legitimacy of personal authority arises from a perception of differences in strength. The authority conveys, the subject perceives, that there is therefore something unattainable in the character of the authority. There is a power, self-assurance, or secret the authority possesses which the subject cannot penetrate. This difference arouses both fear and respect. The combination of these two was captured in the early English sense of the word "dread" and the early French sense of the word "terrible." Hegel expressed this by saying that an authority is perceived to be legitimate when his strength makes him an Other, a person inhabiting a different realm of strength.

A legitimate personal authority is perceived as able to do two things: judge and reassure. Because of his or her inner powers, the authority knows about the subject something the subject does not know. We recall that the fears of being seen through, exposed, shown up, come out of the authority's capacity to judge others. The highest authorities of Mycenaean civilization were seers—literally "lookers-in." In an Ibo tribe the witch doctor can judge the spiritual state of a patient because he is supposed to be able to see into the body. The chief's courage is a standard which makes it legitimate for him to judge the courage of his warriors. He can understand theirs; they cannot understand his—*by definition.* He is the chief. This arbitrary, conventionalized definition of strength and the power of judgement it gives connects authority in an African tribe to a social life as far removed from it as the niceties of precedence in the court of Louis XIV. Society defines classes and castes and types of human difference; these conventions are lived as truths, not as mere labels pasted on something different called "reality."

The powers which make an authority a judge make it possible for him also to give reassurance. He is strong, he knows, therefore he can protect the others. The Roman *auctor* was, in one of his guises, the giver of guarantees; the principle of protection was embodied in the *feudum* contract between the medieval lord and his subjects. In societies without a rigid caste structure, the authority performs a more subtle mission of reassurance. He confirms others, reassuring them that the everyday activities they perform have a larger significance. The subtlety lies in the fact that his sheer presence is confirming, whether or not his subjects are obedient. Miss Bowen defies her father but needs him as a focus, a point of reference, to give her the sense that her erotic life has a resonance beyond the men she involves herself with.

At the heart of these powers is the combination of fear and respect an authority inspires. To lessen the power one must lose fear of the authority. Yet can this be done? One school argues that inspiring fear is the very foundation of the authority's psychological legitimacy.

This was the theme of those famous chapters in Machiavelli's *Prince* in which Machiavelli takes up the question of whether it is better for a prince to be loved or feared. Machiavelli believed there could be no personal authority without fear playing the ruling hand. The prince in need of inspiring fear was one who had overturned an established dynasty or conquered a new territory; he had to transform brute force into authority. The majesty of this new ruler depends on his capacity to create a public image for himself of an unfathomable, superior being, whose displeasure is terrible and whose goodness is unpredictable. The conqueror who contrives this persona will seldom actually have to kill or imprison his subjects; out of fear they will obey of their own accord. A crisis of authority which in any way loosens the bonds of fear will altogether destroy him—like a fatal crack, however small, in an engine. A more moderate view pervades Max Weber's analysis of the charismatic ruler, again a figure who comes to power in overthrowing established regimes, either as a religious prophet or as a revolutionary. As the fear this new leader inspires decreases, his personal authority wanes and becomes absorbed into bureaucracy: Christ inevitably becomes the Church. This bureaucracy is but a faint echo of the passions the personal authority inspired, and the center of those passions, in Weber's view, is awesome fear. This fear creates the essential Otherness of an authority.

If this way of thinking is correct, then a trade-off exists between the psychological legitimacy of an authority and the freedom from fear of his subjects. The less fear you have of an authority, the less respect you have for him. While this might be true of a usurper or a religious prophet, it will not hold good as a general proposition. Fear is a poor basis for creating genuine respect for a parent. More broadly, there are ways of losing one's fear which do not erode one's respect for the authority, but do change one's sense of his or her powers: how the authority ought to protect, reassure, judge. It is this kind of change I wish to explain.

There is a bravado way of losing one's fear of authority. It is flat denial, simple insult. Except the matter is then so quickly settled that nothing has been risked: the employee who prints the negative of his employer as his own ideal; Miss Bowen who tells her father he has no legitimate right to order her love life while needing him more and more. The point at which the legitimacy of an authority can truly be tested is the point at which something other than a yes or a no defines the answer.

It might seem that a less deceptive way to lose one's fear of authority lies in giving oneself over more fully to mortal combat with the authorities. Not ritual rejection, but open warfare. This is the psychological "theory"—if one wants to call it that —of many modern terrorist groups. An act of terrorism against the established order has its real value, supposedly, in rooting out fear of the authorities; each wanton act of violence has its logic in the burden it lifts from the terrorist and his or her audience; nothing need be which can be violated. The great statement of this view occurs in the speech the nihilist Bazarov makes to his companion Arkady in Turgenev's *Fathers and Sons;* here is how the speech ends:

> You aren't made for our harsh, bitter, solitary kind of life; you aren't insolent, you aren't nasty, all you have is the audacity, the impulsiveness of youth, and that is of no use in our business. Your type, the gentry, cannot get beyond noble humility, noble indignation, and that is nonsense. You won't, for instance, fight, and yet you think yourselves terrific. We want to fight. . . . Our dust will eat out your eyes, our dirt will spoil your clothes, you haven't risen to our level yet, you still can't help admiring yourselves, you like castigating yourselves, and that bores us. Hand us others—it is them we want to break. You are a good fellow, but, all the same, you are nothing but a soft, beautifully bred, liberal boy.

This view of what fear is and how it is to be overcome seems to me not only evil but bad psychology. The fear of the authorities Bazarov preaches involves pushing them outside, making them totally external figures who excite nothing of one's own feelings—save disgust. There is a contrary way the fear of authority is overcome, one I would argue is not only more efficacious but also more courageous. It has to do with that process of admission Hegel called an unhappy consciousness; it has to do with taking the images of authority so close to oneself, looking at them so intently, that one loses one's fears of them as mysterious beings, of literally seeing an authority up so close that all traces of mystery are removed.

I am thinking, as an example, of the famous photographs Richard Avedon took of his dying father. The elder Avedon is first photographed before the onset of his illness; he appears a confident, debonair man. Succeeding photographs show his cheeks fall, his eyes protrude from their sockets; the skull seems to shrink. He has his shirt and tie on in most of the photographs; the end is signaled when these signs of being fit for the world disappear and he wears a hospital gown. There is nothing grisly in these pictures; Avedon wants neither to dramatize his father's death nor to hide anything, just to see it. And he has no fear of seeing. Turgenev's character refuses to connect; behind his scorn is still the fear that he will be polluted by contact with the world. No such fear of pollution appears in Avedon's photographs.

The relation between a fear of authority and pollution is a subject Mary Douglas explored in *Purity and Danger.* In some cultures, like that of the ancient Hebrews, the authorities ruled on what was pure and impure for all to eat or drink; in other cultures, like that of the Indian Brahmans, only the bodies of the authorities were themselves pure, and no one else could partake ritually of this purity. Conversely, a priest may be declared illegitimate if his subjects eat food he has declared impure but come to no harm. If there is no danger, there is no authority; the priest has failed to arouse a creditable fear. The Western ideas of rebellion against authority often take the form of performing an impure act; for instance, the Victorians spoke of sexually adventurous daughters as "polluted," and treated homosexuality among their sons as "contagious."

Bazarov's speech calls to our attention a particularly dark connection between authority and fears of pollution. It is that an authority can morally pollute those who come under his or her sway. This fear of moral pollution is that the seductions of authority will make a person soft and pliant; of this Bazarov accuses Arkady. Or the fear is that the pull of authority will pollute a person's sense of rational behavior. In those parts of *The Authoritarian Personality* written by Theodor Adorno, there are presented over and over again images of malign authority—Nazis, Ku Klux Klansmen—raping the minds of followers who are desperate for something absolute and omnipotent to trust but who, away from the presence of the malign authorities, are still rational beings. This dark connection between authority and pollution means that it seems psychologically legitimate to do under the aegis of a Hitler what in a corner of people's minds they know is politically or ethically illegitimate.

Hegel's prescription for these connections between authority and pollution is a radical one. The evil effects of authority can only be combated by getting closer and closer to an authority. The further away that personage is, the more he or she will inspire fear and awe. The closer the authority comes, the less omnipotent the authority can appear. Avedon's photographs are a literal rendering of what "close" means. Psychologically getting "close" to an authority can be as complex as the empathic act of doubling or as simple as a young adult discovering, on becoming a parent, why his or her parents enforced a certain rule. Or it may be a relentless search in a therapy to give reasons to the behavior of parents or lovers who didn't explain themselves. This is the demystifying of authority; differences of strength may remain, but the authority is dispossessed of Otherness—of strength which appears mysterious and unfathomable. Because there is no longer a secret, the authority is not separated by an unbridgeable gulf from his or her subjects. This is what Hegel means by taking an authority inside, getting close to what remains different.

I would like to give some ordinary examples of this loss of fear. One of the accountants described in Chapter One has a lesbian lover:

*Subject:* [She is] so maddening, so passive about little things, and she is like a rock about the real things.

*Interviewer:* What do you mean, like a rock?

*Subject:* She has her reasons, and you know it terrifies me, I can't understand why she wants to change apartments or our vacations, but I always give in, I have to.

*Interviewer:* Why? Are you afraid she'll leave?

*Subject:* Not really, it's just that when she won't tell me about the apartment moving, for instance, she seems to have her reasons, to be in the right.

*Interviewer:* Clara, this sounds bad. So how did you work it out?

*Subject:* Well, it's hard to explain. I mean, we'd gone over everything about the apartment a million times, and about my money from my mother, but finally, well, I began to understand she was afraid I might put up good reasons, and she worried, you know, she worried she'd have nothing left. I mean, here I was being afraid of her when she got all silent, and actually she was afraid of me. So what happened was this. Once I knew she wasn't butching me, and I'm jelly to being butched [slang for abuse by a tough woman], I wasn't so afraid she'd call my number. Well, anyhow the upshot was that I got nicer but tougher, you know. I didn't let myself get hurt and sulk, but I was firmer with her, and I guess that's how we worked it out.

In this instance, silence creates distance and control. At a certain point in a serious fight with her lover, the accountant realized why the silence existed. The language she uses to explain this realization shows how she has drawn the conflict into her own orbit; the other person is no longer alien and cowing. In the following instance, on the contrary, a young woman has instead to destroy a very complete explanation of why she was being controlled by her parents and doctors for a weight problem. She creates a question mark in her relationship with these authorities, she silences them, and that makes her less timid in dealing with them.

*Subject:* As it shows on the records, I weigh 170.

*Interviewer:* And it says here you are five feet eight; is that right?

*Subject:*   Yes. They say it's overweight [her body] by about 40 pounds. "Grossly overweight." (said in a mimicking voice)

*Interviewer:*   Who is "they"?

*Subject:*   Well, my parents and these special doctors for weight problems.

*Interviewer:*   Horrible phrase, "grossly overweight."

*Subject:*   I hate it. Actually I sort of feel okay about how I look. Now I do.

*Interviewer:*   And before you didn't?

*Subject:*   Look, I had it explained up and down to me how serious it was. I went to child shrinks. Fat-farms. The more they explained it to me, the worse I felt . . . and the trouble when you are a fat child is this; you are always trying to please these people telling you there's something wrong. You feel awful about yourself but don't understand what you've done wrong.

*Interviewer:*   I'm surprised you can talk so easily about it.

*Subject:*   Well, about my parents, they got hooked on these fat doctors, so I had to do a lot of explaining. Although it's funny, I dug in my heels and refused to go when I realized my parents were as confused as I was.

*Interviewer:*   How so?

*Subject:*   Look, I didn't know why I was fat, or why it was bad, but I thought they did. When it turned out they were as up in the air as I was, I figured, fuck the whole thing, no more diets, none of it.

What makes these examples so understandable is the means these people used. They had to struggle to learn what they came to know about the authorities. It seems natural in our culture to struggle against authority to change its nature; that is, in itself authority seems fixed, a static force. Contrast this to the self-transforming sense of authority in Ibo culture. As a child, the Ibo possesses no authority, is only a subject. Rites of passage in adolescence imbue the person with equal strength to those who formerly were the protectors. The parents no longer inspire the same fear as they did in childhood, but the legitimacy of the elders is not therefore diminished. Rather, it changes. Its new form is advice rather than command. As the adult Ibo finishes his or her own cycle of parenting, the authority changes again; memories of the tribe's past become his or her source of authority. This is "non-embedded" authority par excellence: what a person's authority is depends on the circumstances of that person's life. Authority exists, but not inflexibly in one form. Illegitimate authority in such a tribal society would be precisely the attempt to freeze the conditions of authority into a single mold. Illegitimate authority, that is to say, would be identified with permanence.

Our society lacks such organized rituals of initiation which transform authority. For us it is necessary to lessen the fear of authority through getting close to it in uncomfortable events of disruption. The discomfort of the servant in getting close is the measure of whether or not the fear is being tested. Conflicts may, of course, harden people into rigid positions. But for both the accountant and the young woman a contrary process has occurred: conflict has transformed the combatant. Unlike Bazarov, they take a real risk in feeling more and more *about* the authority, and this breaks their fear. In *The Functions of Social Conflict,* Lewis Coser has shown how certain kinds of conflict may "integrate" personality structures. Technically what happens in the case of the accountant is that she makes a comparison between her own silence and that of her lover; there are no longer two kinds of silence, one bred of strength, the other of fear. This comparison, made during the course of a hard battle, pulls her together. The young woman deconstructs the explanations her parents make of her own weight problem, and that gives her a certain encouragement; they are as confused as she is. Rejection is the consequence of neither of these acts of breaking fear; a sense of mutuality results, and the persons involved can articulate their needs to people they feel closer to. The lover is still strong, the parents still parents, but no longer overwhelming presences. The term "integration" has a parallel to what Hegel meant by the concept of authority as an "inner" matter, but Hegel sees this inner condition as itself a conflict. Certainly the letter Kafka wrote his father, the letters Madeleine Gide burned, the photographs Avedon took are acts which caused great pain, even though they may have pulled together elements of personality necessary to engage the problem of authority in each person's life. For this reason, Hegel's term—an "unhappy consciousness"— is probably more descriptively accurate.

What Hegel called an evolution of consciousness has so far been our concern. The "data" are intimate experiences of conflict. The transformation of authority through conflict is a possibility in intimate life, nothing more or less, but a possibility with a certain form. This possibility is radically at odds with the way authority is publicly organized now. Both paternalism and autonomy are authority presented as states of being. No inner history, no evolution, is suggested in their imagery. The children of Pullman and Stalin are never expected to grow up; they might be expected to be bad or disobedient, but that is all within a fixed frame of reference.

The reason we know about Hegel's journey at all in intimate life is that the growth and decay of the body, the waxing and waning of parenting, are ineluctable forces which disrupt established relations of authority. At least the possibility exists to learn from these disruptions. No similar possibility exists in public. The accountant whose intimate experience I have described is living in two different worlds at the same time, a private one in which authority remakes itself through productive conflict, and a public one in which authority is static and subject to a negation which is static.

I want to connect the journey of unhappy consciousness to the structure of large-scale institutions. The connection depends on the quality and form of disrupting authority we are able to effect in public life. The bridging of the two worlds is not a matter of superimposing intimate values onto the hard world of power. We can know more about the complexity and morality of authority in private than our institutions allow us to know in public. Why should we be the prisoners of simplicities in public affairs? Only the interests of our masters are served if we do not seek to make the complexities of our consciousness standards for collective experience.

# 5

# Visible, Legible Authority

The work of authority has a goal: to convert power into images of strength. In doing this work, people often search for images that are clear and simple. This search for clear and distinct images of authority, however reasonable, is dangerous.

One of the most repressive beliefs a tyrant can arouse is that everything he does is clear and distinct. Look, what I do is straightforward, it all fits together, nothing is hidden. In other words, how can you resist me? The historian Jacob Burckhardt spoke of the tyrants of the modern age as "brutal simplifiers," and the regimes we think of as authoritarian fit his formula; the Führer and the Duce were embodiments of what it is to be a strong person rather than a competent director of the legal order of government. A person can be simple, clear, and strong all at once, as a big bureaucracy cannot be. By appealing to the virtues of simplicity, authoritarian leaders attempt to wreck or abandon the ordinary machinery of government so that they can rule through force of personality alone. Here is Mussolini's rather rueful comment to a friend about his own struggles to "clear away the brush":

> If you could imagine the effort it has taken me to search for a possible equilibrium in which I could avoid the collision of antagonistic powers which touched each other side by side, jealous, distrustful one of the other, government, party, monarchy, Vatican, army, militia, prefects, provincial party leaders, ministers. . . .

I am a strong man, Mussolini said, because I don't get tangled in these weeds. And here is Hitler, in *Mein Kampf,* on the virtue of a clear image of authority:

> It is therefore the first obligation of the new movement standing on the ground of the folkish world view to make sure that the conception of the nature and purpose of the state attains a uniform and clear character . . . thus the precondition for the existence of a higher humanity is not the state but the nation. . . .

The counterpart to this figure who looms up from the "decadent" morass of bureaucracy is a populace which is aroused by him. But the very measure in which the populace fervently believes in him makes it apathetic about the institutions, with all their mess and pettiness, that he has succeeded in transcending. The key to the success of totalitarian regimes, the political analyst Juan Linz has observed, is the instilling of apathy about the ordinary processes of government in the minds of the citizenry in the name of a higher, clearer order.

This, then, is the danger in the desire for clear images of strength, a danger which knows no national boundaries. Nor can a magic idea make strength clear yet leave people free. Power is relieved of its complexity only by lies about what it is. And yet the impulse to clarify is not, in its inception, diseased. This impulse in modern society is rational and compelling because the dominant images of strength are so deeply unsatisfying. The promises of paternalistic strength are deceptive, humiliating: submit and I will take care of you; how I do so is up to me. The strength of an autonomous person has no nurturance: you need me, I don't need you; submit.

The intimate crises of authority detailed in the preceding chapter are ways in which people attempt to clarify images of strength without losing the sense of complexity. The essence of this intimate knowledge is a connection between authority and time. No one is strong forever; parents die, children take their place; love between adults is not a solid object; authority is not a state of being but an event in time governed by the rhythm of growing and dying. To be conscious of the link between strength and time is to know that no authority is omnipotent. David's *Serment des Horatii,* for instance, depicts this knowledge: the dying leader asks his followers to carry on his life's work. Initially they swear to, and then find that changed circumstances make it impossible for parental truths to endure. The hard truth Hegel has to teach about such knowledge of fallibility in the public world is who will gain it and how. The servant must gain it, and the servant must gain it alone. The master is blinded by his own power; the pleasure of domination makes him too insensitive to recognize that it must come to an end. Even were the master a selfless saint, no person could make a gift of this knowledge to another. The servant must clarify in his mind, then, how another person's strength is limited. The reward of his labors will be that he will lose the fear of authority as omnipotent, and so can begin to set himself free.

The difficulty in translating this intimate knowledge into the political realm is that intimate time and cultural time are not the same. A bureaucracy does not grow and die on the inevitable schedule of the body. Nor is it likely, not to say inevitable, that in government the masters will fall and the people take their place, as parents die and their children become parents. Most of all, consciousness can be puissant in an intimate scene; it is an open question how forceful a weapon consciousness can be for those oppressed by hunger, harsh laws, or intimidation in bringing their masters to heel.

Psychological knowledge of strength cannot, therefore, be

directly translated into a political program. Nonetheless it suggests two criteria of strength, two demands which can be put on the system of public power. These demands may disturb the public order precisely because they are against its grain, because they come from a sphere of life ruled by a different rhythm of time. These demands are that figures of public authority be legible and visible.

"Visible" means that those who are in positions of control be explicit about themselves: clear about what they can and cannot do; explicit about their promises. "Legible" specifies how this open statement could come about. No person in power can be trusted to serve as his own judge and jury. It is the subjects who have to decide what power means; the servants have to read the masters' actions as though trying to make sense of a difficult text. To make power legible in this way was the aim of all the intimate struggles described in the preceding chapter. The act of reading is always a reflexive activity: purging, masking, empathizing, losing one's fear are acts the subjects perform on themselves in order better to see and judge the authorities in their lives.

What I shall explore in this chapter is how the occasions for this reading might occur in public life. They can occur when the elemental structure of power, the chain of command, is disrupted in particular ways. My aim is to show how disrupting the chain of command in these special ways does not create chaos, or destroy the sense that someone with strength is in charge, but rather offers the subjects a chance to negotiate with their rulers and to see more clearly what their rulers can and cannot—should and should not—do. The result of these disruptions is to remove the quality of omnipotence from figures of authority in the chain of command. Connecting authority and disorder is not arcane; it is simply taking seriously the ideal of democracy.

All the ideas of democracy that we inherited from the 18th Century are based on the notion of visible, legible authority. The citizens are to read together; they are to observe the conditions of society and discuss them with one another. The result of this common effort is that the citizens entrust certain powers to the leaders, and judge the leaders on how well they merit that trust. The conditions of trust are to be entirely visible; the leader, Jefferson says, may use discretion, but may not be permitted to keep his intentions to himself. Moreover, reading power and revising its terms occurs only when the people disrupt the regimes which had previously existed and begun to become entrenched. The "normal" processes of voting and the like will not serve. Jefferson's idea of a revolution every generation is well known; in European democratic thought of the 18th Century there is a similar importance accorded to periodic convulsion as the moment in time when the democratic process is strongest; we find this belief in the Abbé Sieyès and in d'Holbach.

The reason the Enlightenment democrats believed authorities could be legible and visible to the people, and that periodic disordering of power would be bearable, was that these thinkers had immense faith in the rational powers of the human race. Whether or not this faith was misplaced, it is certainly true that the Enlightenment democrats discounted how hard is the work of creating images of strength. The conundrums of complex power, the mutual destructiveness of faction, the manipulation of mass belief—these phenomena were assumed to be conquerable if only the inherent rationality of mankind could be released from the shackles of tradition-bound society. The reproach Madison made to these secular believers, in his portions of *The Federalist Papers,* was that they had no idea of the sheer difficulty of democracy, and of the unusual and risky society they proposed to found at a stroke.

In the two centuries since Madison wrote, we have come to see just how fragile is democracy's vision of authority. To say that the people are the source of all authority tells very little psychologically about how authority is made: how, out of the acts of discussion and mutual decision-making, some people are asked to be the protectors of others but forbidden to become their lords. A law can state this will occur, but what makes it humanly possible? The tolerance—indeed, the necessity—of periodic disorder which the Enlightenment democrats envisioned is no longer entertained in law or practice. Societies which are free and democratic in name often put themselves in the paradox of using repressive means to quell disruption in order to "save" democracy.

A structure of power responsive to those who are its subjects; the links in the chain of power discussed and remade during moments of stress; strong persons who arouse limited faith—it may be an impossible, utopian dream, but it is no more than taking seriously the ideals to which most Western societies pay lip service.

## THE CHAIN OF COMMAND

Power between two people is the will of one person prevailing over the will of the other. In the first chapter of this book, we observed ways in which simple obedience is not an adequate measure of the imbalance of will. A person like Miss Bowen can disobey her parents by dating blacks, yet be absolutely dependent on what she knows is her parents' will in choosing lovers; she is disobedient but they are in control. The fantasy of disappearance is a negation which similarly makes one person's will control another's, as does idealized substitution.

The chain of command is the structure by which this imbalance of will can be extended to thousands or millions of people; it is the architecture of power. The principle of building is reproduction: A controls B, B controls C by making A's command his own, C controls D in repeating B's command, and so on. The great analysis of the chain of command by General von Clausewitz (Napoleon's antagonist at Jena and in the Russian campaign of 1812–1813), *On War,* opens with the famous sentence connecting war to the contest of wills: "War is nothing but a duel on an extensive scale." The "extension" occurs through the architecture of the chain of command. The only thing which makes war unlike other forms of power is the use of violence: "War therefore is an act of violence intended to compel our opponent to fulfill our will." Von Clausewitz had a very clear notion that the chain of command was not a simple reproduction at each link of orders from the top. The will of the General dominates: in order for it to be effective, some latitude in the particulars has to be allowed to subordinates in the field. The middle of *On War* is therefore all about what it means to control others along the chain, but not oversee every petty detail. Von Clausewitz observes:

> A constant order of battle, a constant formation of advance guards and outposts, are methods by which a general ties not only his subordinates' hands, but his own in certain cases.

What is impermissible is that the subordinates are free to interpret the basic purposes and design of the General's strategy; this would destroy the chain of command. Control lies in the General's will determining the whole.

It is fitting that this elegant and precise analysis of what power means in a chain of command should have been written by a military man, for the chain of command has its historical origins in warfare. It was the idea which transformed tribes, fighting face-to-face spontaneously, into armies. In Homer's epics we see both tribes and armies at war. The latter are the forces of civilization. The chain of command has disciplined the spontaneous violence of the warriors; in the same measure it has brought forward a new kind of hero, the leader who dominates others not by virtue of his physical strength and courage alone but also by his rational capacity to organize strategy. Thucydides' *History of the Peloponnesian War* shows a schism in the chain of command which then opened up in the ancient world: Sparta, in which the principle is pure and universal, and military and civilian life are indistinguishable; Athens, in which the principles of military control clash with the discussions and uncertainties of the democratic civil state.

Historically, the pure chain of command, such as it appeared in the armed camp of Sparta, is rare. More usually there are breaks in the chain, or many different chains which create a social hierarchy. The *feudum* of the Middle Ages was a broken chain. There was in principle a straight line of descent from kings or great nobles at the top of the pyramid to the lowliest vassal; in point of fact, the contracts of the *feudum* created a patchwork quilt of local obligations. The Burgundian king could rally all his subjects—again in principle—in time of war; practically, he could not issue tax laws to pay for the war which might interfere with the local hereditary relations within a manor. Church and state in the Middle Ages exemplify the relation of different chains; they were wound around each other like a rope but always separable, in terms of duties, privileges, and obligations.

In the modern world, the chain of command as an architecture of power has had an uncertain relation to the market. In theory a market is built not by direction from the top but by competition between antagonists on a relatively equal footing. The great danger, as Adam Smith realized, was that the victors in this competition might press their advantage to destroy their adversaries once and for all—and so destroy the market itself. The advent of vertical and horizontal monopolies, cartels, and government-run businesses is this danger come to life; they are more rigid chains of command than markets. On the other hand, the oil cartels, multinational companies, and government-run industries allow market forces to operate to a limited extent. They do so when the market can still generate some kinds of profit; for instance, the oil cartels want an open international market so that the price of this scarce resource will rise. But when competition gets serious and prices may fall, the cartel clamps down. Smith didn't take seriously the idea that producers could easily cooperate to regulate scarcity and so coherently manipulate the market; supply and demand seemed to him to pull mutually and equally. Thanks to an economy that von Clausewitz would have well understood, they do not.

Even apart from this mixed economy, it would be hard to compare the architecture of power we live in to a compact chain of power on the Spartan model. The Spartans were able to achieve such unity by viewing the world outside their city walls through the red lenses of paranoia. The purpose of power was self-evident; everywhere there were, there could only be, enemies. The legitimacy of the chain of command followed like a mathematical deduction from this paranoia. But in the modern world this legitimacy is problematic. The very fact of international economic combination makes it difficult to convince employees in a particular company that they are engaged in a struggle to the death with competitors, and that therefore the controls exercised along the chain are unquestionably in everyone's interest. Even when there is real cause for paranoia—as among British and American garment industries—it is difficult to make workers more productively obedient by Spartan appeals.

The images of authority analyzed in this book are one way modern organizations, public and private, capitalist and socialist, have tried to make the chain of command internally legitimate. It is the way of universalism. This means simply that a command or control issued at the top has a universal validity in the organization. If it's true, believable, or realistic when the top boss says it, it's equally true all down the line. "I want to do what's best for you" is a paternalistic statement of intention which is universal and which transcends any particular set of facts. The invoking of Chairman Mao's faith in the revolution ahead to justify grain or steel quotas for a particular month during the Cultural Revolution was a similar form of universalism; the sayings, the assurance of good intentions, can be endlessly repeated as they pass from echelon to echelon.

Images of simple autonomous authority are reproduced in a different manner. Simple autonomy means that the expert is understood only by his expert peers. None of the ranks below know how to question him. The dictates of expert authorities pass along the chain as what "they"—the authorities

—have decided is best. Images of complex autonomy are reproduced in the way good intentions are. The British manufacturer quoted in Chapter Three set up a standard of self-sufficiency which could be applied to his nearest associate or to the janitors in the plant. Skills are not the material base of this self-sufficiency; "attitude" is. And attitude, like good intentions, floats free. It is a universal standard by which all may be judged, all may be disciplined, everything explained.

In modern organizations, the control behind either of these images of authority is often masked. Naked power draws attention to itself, influence does not. This veiling of power, built into the foundations of administrative science in the work of Herbert Simon, also oils the links in the chain of command. Memos and directives rationalize rules by recourse to images of expertise, good attitude, or the good intentions of the corporation, but no particular person is responsible for them. They are texts with absent authors, they can be read again and again at each stage in the organization; the meaning repeats down the chain of command, since they have no visible source and apply to the organization as a whole.

The effectiveness of universalism in making the chain of command legitimate is boldly argued by Lenin in his tract *One Step Forward, Two Steps Back:*

> The party link must be founded on formal, "bureaucratically" (from the point of view of the disorganized intellectual) worded rules, strict observance of which alone can guarantee that we are kept from the willfulness and the caprices of the circle [or coterie; R.S.] spirit, from the circle's methods which are termed the "free process of the ideological struggle."

Lenin worried that there would be democratic deformation of the chain of command. Universalism is a way of preventing that. If a general, a party leader, or an industrialist can deal in universals, he wins a kind of omnipotence. Not that he controls everything in the smallest detail, but everything is ultimately under his control because his will is reproduced as accurately as possible down the chain of command.

The question we have to explore, then, is how this universalism can be undermined; the answer seems essentially to lie in disturbing that process of reproduction. But the manner of doing so is in dispute.

## DISRUPTING THE CHAIN OF COMMAND

There are three libertarian strategies for confronting a chain of command. The most extreme is that of the Spanish anarchists: do away with it. The most benign is mutual cooperation between the various ranks in an organization, on the model of the co-determination of industry in West Germany. A third way accepts the fact of hierarchy, but searches out special ways to disrupt it periodically.

The dream of the Spanish anarchists was of a society without hierarchy of power. This belief was tied to a faith in the possibility of living spontaneously—to work, fight, entertain, procreate as one is moved. Because there would be no hierarchy of power, there would be no need for authority, no need for images of the strong and the weak. If taken seriously as a plan for an ongoing society, the idea of an absolute prohibition on the chain of command is indeed sinister. If it were taken seriously, no one would ever need to be obliged to anyone else; in place of social domination one would have placed an omnipotent self responsive only to its own desires. The narrowness of this concept of life has been captured by Giovanni Baldelli, in his remarkable book *Social Anarchism,* as follows:

> A life appears completely meaningless when nothing is felt to depend on it. Not to be the parent, the author and originator, of anything, is to feel oneself out of place in the world, completely gratuitous and supernumerary. It is in the full sense of the word to be unimportant. Thence the craving in most men for some form of authority, that is, for recognition of their importance, for justification of their existence.

Put another way, an iron law of spontaneity would make most human relationships trivial.

A more humane response to the problem of domination through a chain of command are the ideas of cooperation and mutual decision-making which animate the movements for co-determination in the United States (in the auto union most notably) and in various industries in Europe. Co-determination recognizes the elemental necessity for a chain of command. It recognizes the need for coordination, and of the differences in human abilities and strength in a hierarchy. What it refuses to accept is that the power of those higher on the ladder should be absolutely reproduced over those who are lower. Instead, decisions which affect a whole organization should be co-determined by representatives from all echelons: labor, management, the public affected by the organization.

In West Germany this system has been organized legally by the state. There is a works council *(Betriebsrat)* composed of representatives of all workers, excluding management, whose rights are protected by the works constitution law *(Betriebsverfassungsgesetz)*. This council deals with social issues and the internal working conditions of an enterprise. It in turn feeds information and suggestions to the main organ of co-determination, the economic committee *(Wirtschaftsausschuss)* composed of both management and worker representatives. There are also boards of supervision *(Aufsichtsrat)* in the coal and steel industries which use the principle of co-determination. The principle of these arrangements, in the words of the West German Trade Union Federation, is that ". . . in certain sectors of the economy autonomous undertakings operate within the framework of a free market economy system."

The trade union federation recognizes that the plan of co-determination has not been fully realized. Many basic decisions are still taken by those at the top of the chain of command with little interference. A more radical attack on co-determination, by Helmut Schauer, argues that the system is not really democratic at all:

Neither the directly elected representatives on the Board of Supervision, nor those delegated by the unions are in any serious way accountable and controllable. Co-determination merely creates the illusion of popular control of elected representatives. In reality, they are largely independent and easily integrated into the existing functions of management.

Whatever the specific defects of the West German system, there is a problem about all the various strategies based on co-determination. They suppose that arrangements mutually satisfactory to the strong and the weak can be found. Co-determination seeks a consensus which will reduce conflict and tension between the strong and the weak, which will make the chain of command more peaceful by making it more democratic. Thus it is not surprising that many of the advocates of co-determination are upset by findings like those of Josip Obradovic, who in 1965 conducted a thorough study of worker participation in decision-making in Yugoslavia. Obradovic found that the workers who participated in self-managing bureaucracies were far more alienated from their jobs than workers in more traditional settings. The reason is self-evident. These participating workers were confronting the realities of domination built into *any* chain of command, no matter what its ideology, and that confrontation disturbed them. Co-determination is a worthy and dignified enterprise, but it shies away from bringing unresolvable conflicts in the chain of command to the forefront of discussion. There is much that can be learned precisely from periodic experience of those conflicts, learning which can occur via the third strategy for dealing with the domination built into the chain of command.

This third strategy aims at openly confronting the process by which control is reproduced along the chain from A to B to C to D. The aim is in Lenin's scornful phrase, to "democratically deform" these controls as they are reproduced from echelon to echelon. I have found it useful to think about how a chain of command can be deformed by making a connection to a concept in aesthetics, the concept of an image which is put *en abyme.*

This term appears for the first time in modern aesthetics in the journal André Gide kept for 1892. There is an entry in which Gide remarks:

> I am pleased to find, in a work of art, the whole subject of the work transposed down to the scale of its characters. Nothing illuminates the work better, or establishes its proportions more clearly. Thus, in some paintings by Memling or Quentin Metsys a small convex mirror somberly reflects the interior of the room in which the depicted scene is set.

Then he searches for some way to label this process. The little image in the mirror is not an exact replica of the larger scene. The convex mirror in Memling's portraits changes the image it reflects, and Gide believes something of the same thing happens in his own writings:

> What I wanted in my *Notebooks,* my *Narcissus,* and in *The Attempt* is a comparison with that procedure in heraldry which consists of placing a second shield within the first: *en abyme.*

*En abyme* labels the reflections which change the images they reproduce.

This process may seem little more than a precious device, but it was Gide's genius, in his later works, to see its moral dimensions. What if the original image, idea, person is morally corrupt—would the process of putting that original *en abyme* reveal in transmutation the nature of this corruption? This question Gide answers, for instance, in *The Counterfeiters.* A good bourgeois becomes unhappy with the lies which have served him as self-evident principles when he hears the lies repeated, in subtly changed ways, by other people; a father finally apprehends the viciousness of his own life when he sees it reflected, in miniature, purified of any coating of civility, in the little cruelties of his son. The title of the novel is an exact guide to its moral vision: the coins of the counterfeiters reveal the base nature of the original metal.

A reflection which is not quite the original has a social as well as a moral dimension. *En abyme* suggests a method for thinking about how the reproduction of power can be disoriented. The method is to treat controls as propositions rather than axioms at each echelon. A proposition can be validated, disproved, or seen to be both true and false. But if at every point in a link the validity and implications of a rule have to be discussed, then an active, interpretative search for the meaning of power is inaugurated, the activity of authority-making itself. I do not think it is inevitable that if people are given the chance to "democratically deform" controls they will necessarily create chaos; some rules, assumptions, justifications might pass perfectly intact as they are reflected down the chain. But because there are inherently different interests between those who command and those who serve, the probability is great that major issues will not pass down intact.

It is perfectly true that you cannot force people to do what might give them more freedom. It also is true that interpretation of complex phenomena takes up time, is inefficient, creates unhappiness and tension. These are well-worn arguments against the democratic process. It is simply a matter of facing the fact: if one really believes in democratic ideals and accepts the necessity of chains of command at the same time, these confrontations are necessary. They are not evasions, as the strategies of co-determination so often are. The faith I think it reasonable to put in these confrontations comes from the capacity of human beings in their intimate lives to reconstitute authority during periods of crisis. We do not do so inevitably; there are always the risks of the shortcut of simple answers being taken, or of immobilizing disenchantment. But there are particular ways to stage a confrontation so that the fear of strength is lost, the element of omnipotence in particular is put to the test.

Here are five ways the chain of command might be put *en*

*abyme.* The list is not exhaustive, yet gives some indication of the wealth of procedures which might be created.

The first and most basic procedure is to require the use of the active voice in the chain of command. The language of bureaucratic power is often couched in the passive voice, so that responsibility is veiled. A familiar example:

> It has been decided that employees will have to sequence their vacations over the entire summer period, in order to prevent plant production irregularities. Thus it will be necessary for each employee to file with his/her supervisor a statement of projected summer vacation, prioritizing three alternative periods. These will then be coordinated by the supervisory group and a vacation schedule will be assigned each employee.

The use of the passive voice here permits the chain of command to extend itself link after link. "It has been decided" means the decision can be pinned down to no particular person—or, indeed, to no particular level of the organization. A principle has been declared which holds good for the whole; it can be applied in department after department. The decision could be rewritten in the active voice as follows:

> Mrs. Jones, Mr. Smith, Mr. Anderston, and Miss Barker decided to tell employees when they could take their vacations this summer. The reason is that the productivity of the organization is disrupted if everyone is away in August. Jones, Smith, and Barker voted for this decision, Anderston voted against, saying the time necessary to coordinate the vacations of a thousand employees would cost the company as much money in the end as letting them determine in each department when they will be away.

This voice does not suggest that a command exists in the abstract as a universal principle for the organization. The memo shows who was for the decision, who was against it; an employee in a particular department who feels aggrieved can cite the beliefs of a superior who voted against the decision. His immediate boss can, equally, cite the fact that a majority did vote the plan, and what caused them to do so. What then might happen here is that the employee and the boss in the particular department could renegotiate a decision made higher up in the organization, repeating the discussion but not mechanically reproducing its effects. The chain of command would be *en abyme.*

The active voice in writing, so direct, seemingly so simple, is the hardest voice to write. The novelist needs immense confidence in his work to declare "this is," "she felt," "this happened." And in political discourse the effort to speak actively is even harder. So much can be avoided if a master acts absent. In a way he does his subjects a favor too by speaking passively, for they need not come face-to-face with his power and its effects on their lives. If we imagine the simple commandment that in taking a decision who, why, when, and to what end must always be directly stated; if we imagine that at each echelon employees have the right to discuss the declarations of who, why, when, and to what end made in the echelons above, then we are imagining a demanding burden put on all those, masters and servants, in the chain of command. The active voice makes demands, furthermore, because in so many bureaucratic decisions people in power don't know what they are doing. They don't think; it's too confusing; they just go ahead and decide. The use of this active voice at least puts pressure on them to recognize that they made a decision which has to be explained.

The procedure of active-voice control has three phases: explicit statements of who decided, why, when, and to what end; discussion of decisions as they pass along the chain of command; revisability of decisions. This is the work of making authority visible. For a master to discuss his power actively is for him to exert a real and admirable strength; for a subject to enter into the discussion and contest the master is for the subject also a strength. For the control to change out of this confrontation is a "democratic deformation" which also goes by the name of freedom.

Several other practices follow from this basic principle. A rigid chain of command assumes that there are clear categories of subjects to whom controls apply. The voice of power can then make itself legitimate by a seeming appeal to fairness: why do you object? The rules apply evenly to everyone in your position. What makes you so special? The dependents can assert themselves only by arguing that they are exceptions. Moral objectors to war are constantly caught in this pressure; they must continually argue that they are genuinely moved by special religious or personal motives, that they are special cases, in order to be exempt; the substance of their objections, that the war is wrong, falls on deaf ears. Categorizing deflects discourse away from what the powerful are doing to whether a subject making objections is like everyone else.

A second procedure for confronting the chain of command is therefore a discourse about categories. Does a rule really apply to distinct categories? What objections to the substance of the rule have no reference to the evenness with which it is applied? A practical example of this discourse has to do with the practice of promoting and rewarding people by seniority. A number of questions can be asked of this practice: is it fair to couple reward with advancing age? If given the opportunity, workers could easily argue that impersonal rewards ought to be given people to match their family responsibilities, so that those in their fifties and sixties earn less than those in their thirties and forties. Or the question could be posed why only people with special ability are exempt from the seniority principle; this practice, as is well known, tends to divide workers among themselves, so that everybody is angling with management to be recognized as a special case, more deserving than the "normal" workers.

An open discourse about categories means that the category a worker finds himself or herself in can shift as the substance of the rules shifts from topic to topic. For purposes of building retirement income, it might indeed be appropriate that older workers get more retirement credits than younger ones; for opportunities to change jobs within a bureaucracy, age might become irrelevant and some other category be used. This shifting of classification, making several different kinds of chains, is democratic when the subjects participate in the defining process. In the co-determination strategy, they do so through representatives who make coherent plans with management. A more democratic strategy is that the negotiations occur directly, that at each echelon there is freedom to redefine categories as problems arise. At first glance this seems a recipe for inefficiency, but the first glance is misleading.

Many American corporations now conduct themselves at the higher levels through management by objectives. A profit or productive goal is set at the top; the higher echelons of management are left free to organize themselves to meet this goal in whatever way seems best to them. Thus three or four units at the same level of the organization chart doing essentially the same work will be internally organized in entirely different ways, as a result of separate internal discussions, and each unit will continually reorganize itself to meet its objectives. In some branches of the auto industry, the process has been highly efficient; in the textile industry, there have been mixed results with experiments of this kind. But the procedure as a whole has been considered appropriate only at élite levels, because, it is assumed, only managers have the self-sufficiency and competence to work in such a flexible environment. A curious assumption: only the élite are capable of democratic relations.

A discourse about categories leads logically to a discourse about obedience. In a rigid chain of command, "will" refers to both what the superior wants and how he wants it done. As von Clausewitz pointed out, absolutely tyrannical control over all details is a leader's recipe for his own downfall. Moreover, workers who contest one procedure and argue for another are often tinged with disloyalty in the eyes of their superiors: "You didn't do what I said." In order to avoid being branded as disloyal, Robert Schrank has observed, an employee will frequently do things secretly in a different way from what the boss wants in order to do it well; the need to act secretly about what only in the end serves the boss's desires is a principal reason employees come to feel contempt for their employers.

Attempts to bring out in the open different kinds of obedience to meet an employer's desires are perhaps the most familiar device for loosening up a rigid chain of command. Managers of both public and private bureaucracies know there has to be some play and inventiveness in the acts of obedience which meet the superior's desires if the response is to be effective. The question is how much latitude is permitted.

A much more extreme form of shaking the chain of command is role exchange. This is the switching of master and servant to take each other's places when they are in conflict, their desires seem irreconcilable, a compromise appears to both sides as a weak-willed cover-up of their differences, and yet they cannot escape each other. The master and servant temporarily changing positions at this point offers the opportunity for a change in perception akin to the process of doubling described in the preceding chapter. Intellectually, this exchange is perhaps the most interesting way of placing the chain of command *en abyme;* it is like seeing another body called oneself in the mirror.

The notion of role exchange has become an important part of modern theories of "permanent revolution." It has seemed to people like Fanon and the planners of the Chinese state during the Cultural Revolution a way to defeat the growth of an entrenched bureaucracy. The Chinese exchanges have been brutal: scholars sent away from their books to do manual labor, peasants called to the city to run computers, and the like. The Chinese during the Cultural Revolution put themselves in a paradoxical revolutionary position. For the sake of freeing people from the toils of bureaucracy, the Cultural Revolution treated people with contempt for their differences in ability and interest. To be free was to make no discriminations.

A much more sensitive handling of role exchange has occurred in Cuba and in Yugoslavia. The exchanging of roles in these countries has a more educational purpose. The surgeon sees what the problems of the nurse are like; the nurse is trained in surgery—under the doctor's guidance at first, but allowed to take over his or her position subsequently when the circumstances seem appropriate. There is a less benign education that temporary exchanges of role can provide. They can teach a boss the impossibility or irrationality of obeying the very rules he sets out for his employees; equally, they can teach employees exactly why the boss cannot do for them all the things they want him to do. The lesson is what the ineradicable conflict of interests means in a chain of command.

It has always surprised me that Marx's followers took his dream of a person who changes roles in a communist utopia —now poet, now laborer, now industrial worker—to be a pleasurable dream. Once there is any form of power built as a chain of command, this exchange of roles is bound to be in part an education in disappointment. Disillusion is an essential ingredient of empathy: "I thought he could, he might, he should . . ."—all exposed as impossible when once one sees through his eyes. In social life, the exchange of roles, especially in highly developed societies with complex chains of command, is a learning about limits. It may, like the empathic doubling in Kafka's letter, create mutual respect, but it can give little pleasure.

Lastly, the chain of command can be shaken by open discourse about nurturance. Or rather, a modern, non-military chain of command can be shaken up this way, because one of the most avoided subjects of modern society is the relation between being controlled and being cared for.

Paternalism dealt with this relation by making the issue of nurturance non-negotiable. Pullman would tell his workers what was best for them; if they wanted to be cared for, they would obey and leave the rest to him. Nurturance was his gift. Unlike a real parent, he conceived it as his right to give or withhold as he saw fit. The aim of autonomy is to repress the subject of nurturance altogether. When Dodds and Blackman come into conflict, the superior exerts moral controls over his subordinate by acting deaf to appeals for guidance and sympathy.

Nurturance is built into the hierarchical structure of modern bureaucracies in the most impersonal ways. Job benefits, day-care, medical help are all planned according to categories: level in the organization, age, family size, and the like. The *padrone*'s nurturance, in which the dependents come to their boss as the need arises, is considered neither efficient nor dignified. Personal forms of nurturance in large bureaucracies consist largely of sponsoring protégés or of doing people "favors"—both paternalistic forms of support. The idea that people have a right to be nurtured, and that they have the right to negotiate this nurture face-to-face with the powerful, to be neither suppliants nor items in a category, seems unrealistic to us—although in most non-Western societies the right to nurturance is taken for granted and exercised face-to-face.

To negotiate nurturance down the chain of command would be an embarrassing activity. It would require people to say, "This is what I deserve, not because of what I've done for you but because of what I need." Everyone has ideas of his or her just needs, but the needs are kept hidden, or they can be easily suppressed by the question "Why does needing make you deserving?" Justifying one's own needs, asking for support, both psychological and material, is something we have learned to do by indirection. Nurturance is a constant in human affairs; modern Western bureaucracies have not transcended it, but buried it, so that it is most comfortable when it is impersonal, and negotiated face-to-face not by statements like "You must help me" but by more veiled games in which subordinates hope to cajole their superiors into helping them.

All the ambivalence we feel about authority is contained in these impersonal or indirect ploys for nurturance. To declare openly that we need someone else, that we have a right to another's strength, seems to make us most vulnerable, and to give the other absolute power over us. The impersonal provision of benefits in a bureaucracy is in fact a way of universalizing nurturance, removing it far from the realm of direct experience, the variety of personal circumstances. This most human of facts becomes a dry statistic. The effect is to withhold the democratic process from the subject of nurturance.

This is why an open negotiation about nurturance face-to-face at each echelon of the hierarchy seems to me the most disruptive experience which can occur in a modern chain of command. It may well be that the result of these negotiations will be further disappointment: there is nothing one's immediate superiors can do to meet what one perceives to be one's needs. For this discussion to have any real meaning, the employee needs to have the power, which the laws of a democratic state could easily guarantee him, to have the right to appeal. Of course the powerful always wish they could help, but circumstances beyond their control prevent them.... The legal machinery to circumvent these evasions is familiar— ombudsmen and the like. The question is of people losing their shame so that they will avail themselves of these tools. Making the first fact of nurturance a face-to-face encounter seems a reasonable way to lose this shame; the issue must be openly discussed.

These, then, are five ways to disrupt the chain of command, all based on the right and the power to revise through discussion decisions which come from higher up: the use of the active voice; discussion of categorization; permitting a variety of obedience responses to a directive; role exchange; face-to-face negotiation about nurturance. These disruptions are opportunities to connect abstract economic and bureaucratic forces into human terms of strength, strength which is visible and legible. It is by these disruptions that authority-making occurs. And it is by these disruptions that the fear of omnipotent authority might be realistically lessened.

To conclude, something must be said about the larger relationship between authority and anarchism.

In the 19th Century, anarchism, from Godwin to Kropotkin to Bakunin, recognized the positive value of authority, just as does the modern anarchist Baldelli, quoted earlier in this chapter. "But," Bakunin wrote,

I recognize no *infallible* authority, even in special questions; consequently, whatever respect I may have for the honesty and the sincerity of an individual, I have no absolute faith in any person. Such a faith would be fatal to my reason, to my liberty, and even to the success of my undertakings; it would immediately transform me into a stupid slave, the tool of other people's will and interests.

The 19th Century anarchists sought for the conditions of power in which it was possible for a person in authority to be made fallible. Their search was informed by two concerns: a concern for the scale of power; a concern to end domination, like curing the body politic of a disease.

The 19th Century anarchists believed that the smaller the community, the more possible it would be to conduct an open and democratic life. Ten people can talk efficiently, they reasoned; a thousand voices talking at the same time is babble. These quite reasonable assumptions about scale draw on an old tradition in political philosophy; it is a tradition which quantifies the conditions in society necessary for the free give-and-take of opinion, a tradition which originates in Aristotle's writings. Aristotle believed a community should be no larger than a man could shout across so that anyone might hear him. Concern with the scale of social discourse—how many people talking in what size community—appears in Rousseau's *Social Contract;* it was a constant concern of those building new towns in the 19th Century. For instance, the English city planner Ebenezer Howard and the Austrian planner Camillo Sitte experimented in their town planning with ways to combine democratic city institutions with efficient small-scale industries. Histories of anarchism sometimes treat the ideas of Godwin or Kropotkin as strange growths having little to do with the intellectual and cultural life around them, whereas in fact their ideas have a logical place and a long pedigree.

If this concern with scale no longer seems convincing, it is first of all because all the forces of modern industrial society tend so insistently toward combination, large size, and increasingly elaborate forms of control. The more conservative anarchists of the 19th Century were sure that the market forces of society were on their side, that the market would keep the scale of life under control. Whereas in the 20th Century the market does not so much regulate power but is manipulated by the large structures of power. Moreover, the 19th Century anarchists had a faith that size itself would transform the very *quality* of power. But just as one parent can tyrannize one child, the mayor and burghers of a small town can tyrannize a community where everyone knows everyone else. They can, indeed, do so more effectively than the rulers of a large city, for in the town there is nowhere to hide.

This second objection bears on the other anarchist concern of the last century. Bakunin was not "against" power; he never believed, as the Spanish anarchists did, in a society in which everyone acted spontaneously according to the dictates of personal will. But he did make a distinction between power and domination. Domination was power without check, power as an end in itself. From this came his famous denunciation of Marx:

> I wonder how Marx fails to see that the establishment of a . . . dictatorship to perform, in one way or another, as chief engineer of the world revolution, regulating and directing a revolutionary movement of the masses in all countries in a machinelike fashion —that the establishment of such a dictatorship would be enough of itself to kill the revolution and distort all popular movements.

The cure for the disease of domination was the right kind of power, small in scale, mutual in its means, altruistic in its aims. Here, too, the anarchism in whose name Bakunin spoke so eloquently can be reproached for believing in a society which is reborn, in a qualitative purification.

Domination is a necessary disease the social organism suffers. It is built into the chain of command. The chain of command is an architecture of power which inherently does injury to the needs and desires of some at the will of others. There is no way to cure this disease; we can only fight against it. There can be partial, important victories; it is possible to struc-ture the chain of command so that controls are not omnipotent and universal. It is possible to prevent the alchemy of absolute power into images of strength which are clear, simple, and unshakeable. It is possible for the subordinates to see themselves as more than hopeless victims. Authority can become a process, a making, breaking, a remaking of meanings. It can be visible and legible. Modern anarchism ought to be conceived as purposive disorder introduced into the house of power; this is the hard, uncomfortable, often bitter work of democracy.

# 6

# Authority and Illusion

The fear of being deceived by authority is perhaps the best way to summarize the attitudes of negation explored in this book. The deceptions of totalitarian regimes are the most clearly etched. They are deceptions about the timelessness of authority: the Nazis used the image of a state enduring a thousand years to justify absolute power. They are deceptions in which nurturance legitimates uninhibited power: Stalin used the image of his own boundless strength and love for the people to exact from them absolute submission. Moreover, totalitarian regimes refuse to acknowledge anything contingent or accidental to be real; everything the state does has a reason.

The fear of being deceived by authority in free societies is equally realistic, but the realities of deception are different. Pullman deceived his workers by declaring he would take care of them and meet their needs; unlike Stalin, when their needs clashed with his interests, he simply withdrew the offer of care rather than force them to accept it. The union of power and care we hear in the speeches of our leaders is false. No religion lays it upon the Caesars as a duty before God. It is instead like a decoration which one can easily strip off a cake. We condemn the unreality of what should be the only moral foundation of power by calling this union "pure rhetoric." The autonomous figure seems simply self-enclosed: nothing proffered, no deception. But this too is not the case. His influence can be organized bureaucratically into forms of psychological manipulation. As a role-model, he offers an illusory view of what freedom is like. He is not free from others; he is only freed from dealing mutually with others by arousing feelings of shame and inadequacy in them. A controller of others who appears disinterested: perhaps the ultimate deception.

The word "deception" is a loaded one. If we take it to mean an intent on the part of the powerful to deceive, we would have a picture of those in control as Machiavellian artists. This paranoid vision of authorities who know exactly what they are about requires too much genius among the master classes to be convincing. Indeed, it is precisely because the strong believe in themselves and in what they do that they become creditable in the eyes of others. Deception which occurs without a conspiracy to deceive is properly called illusion. Illusions are deployed systematically, in norms of behavior and belief; they can be shared by masters and servants.

To expose the illusions and the potency of authority became the goal of the negative spirit born in the French Revolution; it was a determination, in Hegel's words, to drive out "the master within." This resolve not to be duped by the appearances of the authorities can have the paradoxical effect of tightening the bond between master and servant. It did so in the case of the accountants bent on exposing the fact that their boss was not the leader a person in her position should be; they needed her negative to see the positive image of authority they wanted. It did so in the case of Blackman and Dodds. Dodds called Blackman's insensitivity to account, and became ever more enmeshed in eliciting from his superior some signs of recognition and approval. Driving out the illusions of the master within can also be a deadening process, in which a depressed passivity follows the act of exposing the claims of the authorities. It did so in the case of the rebellious Pullman workers. Above all, rejecting the moral dictates of another person may build a barrier of transgression which makes it safe to depend on that person in other ways, as it did for Miss Bowen. The claim of authority is always one of personal superiority based on strength. The claim of superiority may be exposed as an illusion, and yet in these various ways the strength is still felt.

Much of the modern literature on authority, from Orwell's *1984* to Huxley's *Brave New World*, presents the belief that to escape from the spell of authority itself is to be free. We have difficulty imagining authority as a sense of strength and weakness we build. The impact of the culture of negation has been to disconnect the making and breaking of authority we do in private life from suggesting anything about public affairs. In public, authority seems external, a force to be confronted. Exposing the illusions of authority has not, in sum, led us to imagine new forms of authority in society, to create after we have negated.

Perhaps the most radical analysis of the relation of authority and illusion in modern literature is Dostoevsky's parable of the Grand Inquisitor in *The Brothers Karamazov*. The parable has two dimensions: what the Grand Inquisitor argues, and the consequences of his argument. In the parable, Christ returns to Seville in the 16th Century; the Grand Inquisitor encounters Christ on the street, surrounded by a crowd for whom He has performed miracles. So great is the worldly authority of the Grand Inquisitor that the crowd bows before him and allows him to arrest their God. At midnight the Grand Inquisitor appears in Christ's prison cell, to explain why he has imprisoned the God he too serves, and why he will burn Christ the next morning.

With great anger, the Grand Inquisitor accuses Christ of having offered the people a vision of authority and freedom combined. It was inhuman of Christ to do so, because the people cannot bear the burden of this combination. "I tell you man has no more agonizing anxiety than to find someone to whom he can hand over with all speed the gift of freedom with which the unhappy creature was born."

The Grand Inquisitor's position is more subtle than La Boétie's, whom we saw in Chapter Four argue that voluntary servitude arose because people are lazy and consumed only by the desire for secure, petty pleasures. "Man is born a rebel," the Grand Inquisitor says. Undisciplined, greedy, out for himself only—a Hobbesian animal. Yet this rebelliousness is self-destructive; the Hobbesian animal cannot control even himself. It is mutually destructive; the animals will kill off each other, and no one will be left. Thus they go in search of some person or principle who stands above themselves, who will put an end to this terrible license which is their freedom. In perhaps the most famous passage of the parable, the Grand Inquisitor declares:

> . . . Man seeks to worship only what is incontestable, so incontestable, indeed, that all men at once agree to worship it all together. For the chief concern of these miserable creatures is not only to find something that I or someone else can worship, but to find something that all believe in and worship, and the absolutely essential thing is that they should do so *all together.*

Something incontestable and certain, something which brings people together: this is the bond of authority. The more people search for human relations which are solid like the stones of a church, the more people will abandon their freedom—and this, proclaims the Grand Inquisitor, is as it should be.

Christ's sin, therefore, was to encourage man to develop in himself a better strength than the licentious strength with which he was born; it was a sin of nurturing man, of setting an example. The Hobbesian animal cannot learn. Worldly authorities must do for him what he cannot do for himself. "Miracle, mystery, and authority"—that is, higher, repressive authority—these are "the only three forces that are able to conquer and hold captive forever the conscience of these weak rebels for their own happiness." Authority is founded on the illusions of miracle and mystery, and they are necessary illusions.

The Grand Inquisitor's argument is an attack on the very effort to expose the mystery and illusions of higher authority, no matter what those mysteries and illusions are. Negation, in Dostoevsky's view, is man's attempt to crawl back to his primitive nature as a free, desiring animal. *Any* illusion which represses that nature is legitimate. Taken alone, the Grand Inquisitor's argument embodies what David Magarshack has called the atavism of Dostoevsky, his horror of the spirit of disbelief in the modern world, his faith in faith for its own sake. Disbelief in authority will never bring back this freedom, because when all is said and done, man does not want to be free. Man only wants to imagine that he would like to be free.

But, as in so much of Dostoevsky's writing, the legend of the Grand Inquisitor is more convoluted than the political program the author puts forward. The second dimension of the legend appears when the Grand Inquisitor concludes his argument by declaring that he has given himself over to the service of the Devil in order that he, and others in positions like his, may keep mankind from destroying itself. Christ has throughout the Grand Inquisitor's speech said not a word. Now, at its end, his only response is to lean forward and give the Grand Inquisitor a kiss. The Grand Inquisitor is moved. Despite all his arguments, he opens the door of the prison to set Christ free. And Christ does not refuse; he does not remain to be sacrificed a second time, but walks out the door of the prison and disappears from the face of the earth. Who has convinced whom? Has God's love triumphed over the logic of repression, or has the spokesman of the Devil finally made God face the facts?

The only answer to a mystery is another mystery, Dostoevsky remarks elsewhere, and that comment, put in a more concrete form, elucidates this second dimension of the parable of the Grand Inquisitor. The only answer to the Grand Inquisitor is imagining a response outside his terms. That is the response of the Christ in Dostoevsky's parable. Whether or not the logic of repression is finally rejected depends upon how dissonant and how pertinent the response can be, like a painter seeing a whole new landscape by changing the position of his easel.

It was in thinking about the ambiguity of this parable that I began to wonder how the rhythms of authority in intimate life might serve as a response to the illusions of authority and their negation in public life. Authority as a constant process of interpretation and reinterpretation makes sense in intimate affairs; it does not in public. There are structural reasons for this; the rhythm of growth and decay in a life is not the rhythm of growth and decay of society. There is an unbridgeable gap —or, to put it positively, each of us can re-imagine authority privately as we cannot in public. We have a principle by which to criticize society based not on abstract deduction about justice and right but on our intimate knowledge of time.

The culture of negation has blocked this criticism by making us distrustful of the work of imagination in public. For instance, there is a connection between Kafka's letter and the problems of mutual recognition in a factory; the connection can only be made in metaphor. The metaphor is different in its very essence from a metaphor of domination like paternalism. Kafka's idea of the connections between father and child is based on the shifts in their relations. Paternalism drew on this connection to present a picture of a fixed, static relationship. In imagining what Kafka's letter means about factory life, we are comparing experiences out of scale, making both intimate and impersonal life more complex by the act of comparison.

The fear of imagination in politics comes from the fear of illusion. It is like refusing to use a tool at all because it can be misused. The dominating metaphors of paternalism, again, made Pullman's workers fear the opposite metaphors put forward by Debs's socialists. A generation ago it was the fashion to explain Nazism in terms of "mythomania." The historian Salvemini spoke of Nazism as a "hideous poetry," and wondered if the masses were strong enough to one day look at power for what it was without the aid of poetry at all. Of course we can never in fact stop using metaphors, allegories, or similes; we would cease to use our symbol-making powers. But we can become so self-conscious and distrustful of these powers that we strive to repress them when we notice them.

Belief in visible, legible authority is not a practical reflection of the public world; it is an imaginative demand placed on that world. It is also an idealistic demand. To ask that power be nurturing and restrained is unreal—or that, at least, is the version of reality our masters have inculcated in us. Authority, however, is itself inherently an act of imagination. It is not a thing; it is a search for solidity and security in the strength of others which will seem to be like a thing. To believe the search can be consummated is truly an illusion, and a dangerous one. Only tyrants fill the bill. But to believe the search should not be conducted at all is also dangerous. Then whatever is, is absolute.

# Index

## ABOUT THE AUTHOR

Richard Sennett was born in Chicago in 1943 and took his bachelor's degree at the University of Chicago and his Ph.D. at Harvard. He is the author of *Families Against the City, The Uses of Disorder, The Hidden Injuries of Class* (with Jonathan Cobb), and *The Fall of Public Man.* He is the founder of The New York Institute of the Humanities at New York University, a research center for scholars and writers; a Visiting Fellow at the Institute for Advanced Study in Princeton; and University Professor of the Humanities at New York University.

## VINTAGE POLITICAL SCIENCE AND SOCIAL CRITICISM